The Last Word
on Guidance

The Last Word on Guidance

Phillip D Jensen
&
Tony Payne

ANZEA

St Matthias Press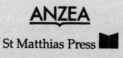

© Phillip D Jensen & Tony Payne 1991

ANZEA BOOKS are published by
ANZEA PUBLISHERS
3-5 Richmond Rd
Homebush West, NSW 2140

St Matthias Press
PO Box 225
Kingsford, NSW 2032

St Matthias Press UK
PO Box 65
London SW20 8RL

ISBN 0 85892 501 X

Typeset by St Matthias Press

Printed in Australia by Griffin Press Ltd

Contents

The First Word

Christians have long been fascinated with how God guides. They have battled with questions like: What is God's will for my life? Is it general, special or both? How should I discern his voice and respond?

In one sense, it is little wonder that Christians have been so interested in guidance, because decision-making is one of the constant burdens of our existence. Whenever we 'do' anything, we make a choice. We cannot avoid it. We face decisions at every point of our lives—from whether to walk against the DON'T WALK sign, to which car to buy.

Choosing is unavoidable, and so are the *consequences* of our choices. Every decision we make has its repercussions—some of them predictable; others completely unexpected. Every time we make a choice, we also choose a whole set of consequences, and sometimes these consequences can change our lives. They can affect our families, our friends, and even the whole of society.

The unfortunate truth is that we aren't very well equipped for making decisions. Unlike God, we aren't all-knowing. We are always unaware of some of the factors affecting our decisions—we don't have all the information at our disposal. I don't know everything about my girlfriend—so how can I be sure that she will make a good wife? The things I don't yet know about her may be the very things that will ruin our marriage!

What is more, we can't control the outcomes that flow from our decisions. Unlike God, we aren't all-powerful. We can't even put all our decisions into effect.

Choosing is hard. We blunder through life without all the information that we need to make decisions. We do our best to make good choices, but are sometimes unable to, and are forced to suffer the consequences and to inflict them on our loved ones.

We aren't even capable of picking which decisions are the important ones. I may think, for example, that whether I concentrate on science or humanities in my later years at high school will be very important. It will determine the course of the rest of my life, so I think at the time. I spend weeks, even months, weighing up all the alternatives and labouring over the decision. However, my choice to play football one Saturday morning turns out to be far more significant. A scrum collapses, I suffer brain damage, and my academic career is over.

We never know which of our decisions will turn out to be vital or even significant. Sometimes, the most trivial decision can have the most profound consequences.

It's a depressing scenario. Perhaps you are already regretting the decision to read this book.

Is God any help?

Almost instinctively, Christians know that God should be able to help us in our decision-making. However, few Christians seem able to get that help from God. For them, God only complicates the decision-making process.

They sense that God has a plan for them, and that he wants them to discover that plan and put it into effect. This only makes choosing harder. They not only need to weigh up all the 'earthly' factors, but they also have to try to discern God's will. For most, this leads to uncertainty and anxiety. For some, it leads to bitterness and regret as they live their lives in the belief that they have missed God's will and must be content with his 'second best'.

What *is* God's plan for us? How do we find it? How does he communicate it to us? Is God concerned with the trivial details of life (such as what sort of car we buy), or is he only interested in the 'big' decisions like marriage and career? What if I should step outside God's will for my life?

In the pages that follow, we have some good news for you. God *does* promise to guide us and, believe it or not, this is meant to reassure us and remove anxiety. He does have a plan, and we have a part to play in it, a part that is clear and easily discernible. If only we understood God's plan, and the part he has given us to play in it, we could face decision-making under God's guidance with joy and confidence.

Such is the purpose of this book (with its seemingly arrogant title): to outline God's will for our lives, how he guides us in it, and what we are to do in response. I hope that by the end, you will see that the title is not as arrogant as it first appears.

PART ONE
The Grand Design

2

O Thou Great Jehovah

For over two hundred years, Christians have been singing:

> Guide me, O thou great Jehovah,
> Pilgrim through this barren land:
> I am weak, but thou art mighty,
> Hold me with thy powerful hand...

We look to God to guide us, just as he guided the children of Israel out of Egypt, across the desert and into the Promised Land.   The Exodus is a marvellous picture of God guiding his people.

Our hymn writer (the unmistakable Welshman, William Williams) rightly applies the Exodus to us as Christians. God leads us through 'this barren land' until we 'tread the verge of Jordan' and land 'safe on Canaan's side' (that is, in heaven). God's character and plans have not changed. He is still a guiding God.

The first step towards understanding God's guidance is to understand the guiding God. We need to explore his character and the way he achieves his plans before we can tackle the nitty-gritty issues we are all so interested in. If we understand God—what he's like, what motivates him, and what his plans are—we will be well on the way to understanding his guidance.

God, the Sovereign Creator

The God revealed to us in the Bible is the Sovereign Creator God of all the world. He made it all. He owns it all. He rules it all.

As the Creator, he continues to create and sustain all things, down to the smallest detail:

> He makes springs pour water into the ravines;
> it flows between the mountains.
> They give water to all the beasts of the field;
> the wild donkeys quench their thirst.
> The birds of the air nest by the waters;
> they sing among the branches.
> He waters the mountains from his upper chambers;
> the earth is satisfied by the fruit of his work.
> He makes grass grow for the cattle,
> and plants for man to cultivate—
> bringing forth food from the earth:
> wine that gladdens the heart of man,
> oil to make his face shine,

and bread that sustains his heart.
                                    Psalm 104:10-15

Jesus expresses this all-embracing care of God for his creation in a striking way:

> Are not two sparrows sold for a penny? Yet not one of them will fall to the ground apart from the will of your Father. And even the very hairs of your head are numbered. So don't be afraid; you are worth more than many sparrows.
>   Matthew 10:29-30

God rules and sustains and replenishes his world down to the most intimate detail. And this is the God who guides his people.

The guidance given to the Israelites in the Exodus was the guidance of the Sovereign Lord of Creation. The plagues, the Red Sea crossing, the manna, the quail, the water from the rock, the voice from Sinai—the whole story bears the marks of the Creator, ruling over his world in order to achieve his purposes for one particular nation.

This continues to be God's relationship with his people. When Israel was in captivity in Babylon, God the Creator promised to rescue them in his own powerful and extraordinary way. He decided to use the pagan king Cyrus as his 'messiah' to rescue Israel from Exile. And if the Israelites felt that this was a rather unorthodox way to save them, God had a word for them:

Woe to him who quarrels with his Maker,

to him who is but a potsherd among the potsherds
on the ground.
Does the clay say to the potter,
'What are you making?'
Does your work say, 'He has no hands?'
Woe to him who says to his father,
'What have you begotten?'
or to his mother,
'What have you brought to birth?'
This is what the LORD says—
the Holy One of Israel, and its Maker:
Concerning things to come,
do you question me about my children,
or give me orders about the work of my hands?
It is I who made the earth and created mankind
upon it.
My own hands stretched out the heavens;
I marshalled their starry hosts.
I will raise up Cyrus in my righteousness:
I will make all his ways straight.
He will rebuild my city and set my exiles free,
but not for a price or reward, says the LORD Al-
mighty.

Isaiah 45:9-13

God, the creator and ruler of the universe, can and
does use everything to rule and guide his people—
donkeys speak, staffs turn to serpents, and bushes
burn without being consumed (see Numbers 22,
Exodus 7, Exodus 3).

All things, including the hearts of men and
kings, are in his hand:

A man's steps are directed by the LORD.
How then can anyone understand his own way?

Proverbs 20:24

> The king's heart is in the hand of the Lord;
> he directs it like a watercourse wherever he
> pleases.
>
> Proverbs 21:1

God, the Shepherd of His People

One of the most familiar, and yet most extraordinary, ideas in the Bible is that God—the Sovereign, Creator God we have just been considering—should choose to enter into relationship with sinful human beings. It is astounding. It is like the President of the United States deciding to befriend a cockroach.

The Bible describes this extraordinary relationship between God and his people as being like a shepherd with his sheep. In Psalm 80:1, God is described as the 'shepherd of Israel, you who lead Joseph like a flock'; and there are a numerous references like this (e.g., Psalm 77:20; Isaiah 40:11; Isaiah 63:11). The most well known, of course, is Psalm 23, which expresses the same idea more personally. God will not only guide the nation, he will also shepherd individuals:

> …he leads me beside quiet waters,
> he restores my soul.
> He guides me in paths of righteousness
> for his name's sake.
>
> Psalm 23:2-3

The leaders of Israel were also called 'shepherds'.

Their responsibility was to lead and guide the
people under God's direction. The tragedy was
that Israel's leaders were often derelict in their
duty. In Ezekiel 34, we read about their negligence
and how, as a result, the people were 'scattered
because there was no shepherd, and when they
were scattered they became food for all the wild
animals' (Ezekiel 34:5). God promises that he himself will come and tend his people, rounding up
the strays, and caring for the weak and hungry.

In light of this passage, we see the significance of
Jesus being the 'good shepherd. In John 10, Jesus
paints a graphic picture of himself as the good and
faithful shepherd who knows his flock by name
and leads them to safety: 'My sheep listen to my
voice: I know them, and they follow me' (John
10:27). The image is taken up elsewhere in the New
Testament, such as in Matthew 9:36, where Jesus
has compassion on the crowds because 'they were
harassed and helpless like sheep without a shepherd' (see also Hebrews 13:20; 1 Peter 2:25; 5:4;
Revelation 7:17).

God relates to his people as a Shepherd to his
sheep. And we need to be under no illusions about
how shepherds guided their sheep in the ancient
world. They had a long staff, the shepherd's
crook—and it wasn't just for leaning on—it was
for whacking their sheep to keep them in line.
We tend to have a very sentimental view of shep-
herding. We think that shepherds just mosey up
to the sheep and gently rub them on the back

and ask them if they'd mind stepping this way.
Shepherds aren't like counsellors—they *lead* their
sheep; they show them where to go and give them
a prod in the right direction if they're slow to get
moving.

This is the relationship of God with his people.
He shows them the way and guides them along it.

God, the Planner

In understanding the God who guides, we also
need to realise that he *makes plans*. The Bible does
not see history as a succession of meaningless,
random events. The God of the Bible is the Lord of
history, who draws up a plan and then pursues it
to completion. God guides according to a plan.

This plan of God is explained in several parts of
Scripture. It is foreshadowed in the promise to Eve
that her seed will crush the serpent's head (Gen
3:15). It is foretold to Abram when he is called by
God (Gen 12:1ff) and reiterated when the sign of
circumcision is given (Gen 15, 17). It is established
by the covenant with Moses and the people of
Israel (Exod 19-23). It is further elaborated to
David (2 Sam 7) and through Jeremiah (Jer 31).
And it finds its fulfillment in Christ (Matt 5:17-20;
2 Cor 1:20) and his people (1 Pet 1:9-10; Eph 1:3-10).

This plan of God covers centuries of human
history. Abraham is told some 400 years in advance that his descendants will be captive in Egypt

and then rescued by God and taken to the Promised Land. God declares that all this will happen; and it does, because God's word is as certain and reliable as the rain that waters the earth:

> It will not return to me empty but will accomplish what I desire and achieve the purpose for which I sent it.
>
> Isaiah 55:11

The New Testament events are likewise under God's control and part of his great plan. Jesus died to redeem us 'when the time had fully come' (Gal 4:4). There is a sense of historical necessity about what Jesus came to do. Even though it involved the brutal execution of an innocent man, Jesus' crucifixion was part of the grand design. It had to happen. Note the little word 'must' as Jesus tells his disciples about what will soon take place:

> He then began to teach them that the Son of Man must suffer many things and be rejected by the elders, chief priests and teachers of the law, and that he must be killed and after three days rise again. He spoke plainly about this, and Peter took him aside and began to rebuke him.
>
> Mark 8:31-32

Peter didn't understand. How could it possibly be part of God's plan for the long-awaited Christ to suffer humiliation and death at the hands of Israel's leaders? It was inconceivable.

However, after Jesus' death and resurrection,

Peter understood that God uses even the inconceivable to achieve his purposes. On the day of Pentecost, he had this to say to the assembled Jews:

> This man [Jesus] was handed over to you by God's set purpose and foreknowledge; and you, with the help of wicked men, put him to death by nailing him to the cross.
>
> Acts 2:23

The details of God's plan need not worry us at the moment. They are very important, but we will pursue them in our next chapter. What is important to note at this point is that God has a plan and he works—sovereignly and irresistibly—to achieve it.

Direct Statements

Having looked at the character of God as the Sovereign Creator, the way he relates to his people as Shepherd, and the cosmic historical plans he makes, we already have a solid basis for expecting God to guide us. However, it also worth noting briefly that there are some direct statements in Scripture that God will guide. These statements are few in number, but they are there.

In Psalm 25, for example, David pleads with God to protect him from his enemies. Based on his trust in God as his Saviour, David declares his confidence that God will guide the humble:

> He instructs sinners in his ways,
> He guides the humble in what is right
> and teaches them his ways…
> Who, then, is the man that fears the LORD?
> He will instruct him in the way chosen for him.
> He will spend his days in prosperity,
> and his descendants will inherit the land.
> The LORD confides in those who fear him;
> he makes his covenant known to them.
>
> Psalm 25:8-9, 12-13

There are similar ideas expressed in Psalm 32:8 and in the well-known passage in Proverbs:

> Trust in the LORD with all your heart
> and lean not on your own understanding;
> in all your ways acknowledge him,
> and he will make your paths straight.
>
> Proverbs 3:5-6

God undertakes to lead his people. As the Sovereign Creator, he has the power to do it; as our Shepherd, it is the way he relates to us; and as the Supreme Planner, he knows where he wants to take us.

This last point is crucial. We must understand *where* God is guiding us. God has a plan, a grand design, that he has been unfolding since before the creation of the world. What is this plan? Where is he taking us? Where does the journey end?

We have already touched on what this plan entails, and our next step is to look at it in more depth.

3

Where to, Moses?

The Israelites were none too happy with Moses. He may have rescued them from slavery in Egypt, but where was he taking them? Freedom from slavery was one thing; freedom to starve in the desert was another! So they grumbled—repeatedly (see Exod 14:11ff, 16:3; 17:3). 'Where are we going? Will it be any better than Egypt? Will there be leeks and onions there? Will we ever get there?!'

Of course, it was not Moses who had rescued and guided Israel. It was the Lord who had saved them. It was the Lord they were doubting. They did not know or trust God's plan for them. They preferred the familiar security of slavery in Egypt.

As we undertake our Christian 'walk' (to use a well-worn biblical term), we often have similar questions. Our interest is personal. It's all very well to talk about the great events of salvation history—the creation, the covenants, the redemption in Jesus, the return of the Lord—but (understandably) we want to know where God is taking *me*? Where is my life heading? Do I have any assurance that I'll get there? What is my role on the journey?

We have already seen that God promises to guide us. His character, his relationship with us, his plans and his direct promises all speak of him as our guide. We now need to look more closely at the details of the plan.

There are many ways we could do this, and the number of Bible passages we could look at is immense. To make the task manageable, we have selected some key passages of Scripture which summarise God's great plans in terms that include the individual Christian believer.

Destined for Sonship

In the opening verses of Paul's letter to the Ephesians, we find a great thanksgiving to God for the blessings which are ours in Christ:

> Praise be to the God and Father of our Lord Jesus Christ, who has blessed us in the heavenly realms with every spiritual blessing in Christ. For he chose us in him before the creation of the world to be holy and blameless in his sight. In love he predestined us to be adopted as his sons through Jesus Christ, in accordance with his pleasure and

will—to the praise of his glorious grace, which he has freely given us in the One he loves. In him we have redemption through his blood, the forgiveness of sins, in accordance with the riches of God's grace that he lavished on us with all wisdom and understanding. And he made known to us the mystery of his will according to his good pleasure, which he purposed in Christ, to be put into effect when the times will have reached their fulfilment—to bring all things in heaven and on earth together under one head, even Christ.

Ephesians 1:3-10

Here is a passage which speaks about God's plan in grand terms, and gives us some insight into our place in the scheme. Paul thanks God for our election (v 4), our adoption (v 5), our redemption (v 7) and our understanding (vv 8-9). Paul praises God because all this is God's work. God has accomplished all this in his love and grace through Jesus.

We should note particularly the purpose for which all this is done. It comes out in several of the verses:

- in v 4, we are chosen to 'be holy and blameless in his sight';
- in v 5, we are predestined to be 'his sons';
- in v 10, God's ultimate purpose is to 'bring all things in heaven and on earth together under one head, even Christ'.

Here is the goal or destination of our lives: to be

under Christ. The Christian has the special privilege of already being submitted to Christ as a child of God, holy and blameless in his sight. And when the times have reached their fulfilment, this process of submission will be completed. All things will be placed under Christ's headship—all things in our lives and in heaven and on earth.

If that is the destination, how will we travel there? By God's gracious mercy and love. God in his rich grace has sent his Son to provide redemption, the forgiveness of sins.

The children of Israel were saved from death by the blood of the passover lamb. They were purchased out of slavery in Egypt and led by God to the Promised Land. Christians are saved by the blood of the Passover Lamb, Jesus. We are purchased out of slavery (to sin) and led by God to that great day when we will be finally and perfectly submitted to Christ.

Destined to Inherit

Like Paul in Ephesians 1:3-10, Peter begins his first letter by praising God for his great blessings to us:

> Praise be to the God and Father of our Lord Jesus Christ! In his great mercy he has given us new birth into a living hope through the resurrection of Jesus Christ from the dead, and into an inheritance that can never perish, spoil or fade—kept

in heaven for you, who through faith are shielded
by God's power until the coming of the salvation
that is ready to be revealed in the last time.

1 Peter 1:3-5

We have been born again through Jesus because
of God's great mercy. Again, we are told the
destination of the journey—we have a living hope
or an 'inheritance' that will one day be ours.

Peter's readers would not have missed the
loaded meaning of the word 'inheritance'. It is a
very Old Testament way of talking about the Promised Land. The land was Israel's inheritance, and
each Israelite had his own personal share, his own
inheritance. The new and living hope is that Christians also have an inheritance, but one far superior
to the one the children of Israel received.

Our inheritance can never 'perish, spoil or fade'
and it is kept in heaven. Ours is a permanent,
undefiled inheritance with God in heaven, and we
are shielded by God's power until such time as
we claim it.

It is like a bank account. Our money is kept there
for us, and elaborate precautions are taken to ensure that the money is secure. But even better,
imagine if the bank manager hired a special security guard to accompany us to the bank so that
we could collect our funds. God is our Bank Manager—he keeps our inheritance for us in heaven
and guards us as we journey on our way to
inherit it.

Here is a clear promise about our destination in

life and how we will get there. We are on our way to heaven, and God will personally ensure that we make it!

Destined for Glory

To cast further light on God's plan, we now turn to a favourite passage for many Christians:

> And we know that in all things God works for the good of those who love him, who have been called according to his purpose. For those God foreknew he also predestined to be conformed to the likeness of his Son, that he might be the first-born among many brothers. And those he predestined, he also called; those he called, he also justified; those he justified, he also glorified.
>
> Romans 8:28-30

This is great news, especially for Christians. 'In all things' God works for our good, that is, for 'those who love him, who have been called according to his purpose'. But what does 'for our good' mean?

The following sentence gives the answer. We know that God works 'in all things' for our good because he has 'predestined [us] to be conformed to the likeness of his Son'. In other words, 'our good' equals becoming like Jesus. It means becoming what we were created to be—the image of God, in harmony with our creator, our society, our world and ourselves. This is 'our good'.

Becoming like Christ is the ultimate 'good', but that doesn't mean that it will be easy. Jesus, after all, was the 'man of sorrows', the man who suffered death on a cross. Becoming like him means becoming acquainted with grief and suffering and yet remaining obedient to the end. To say that God works in everything for our good does not mean that he will remove all pain and suffering from our path. On the contrary, if becoming like Christ is the 'good' that God is working for, then pain and suffering will almost certainly come our way. And through that pain and suffering, God will work in his sovereign way to mould us into the shape of Jesus.

This, then, is our destination, our promised land: to be conformed to the image of Jesus. Again we might ask: How will we get there?

Romans 8 reassures us that nothing in the circumstances of life can thwart God's plan to make us like Christ. The sufferings of this world are nothing compared with the glory that is to come (v 18), and eventually all suffering will be done away with (vv 19-23). In the meantime, nothing can separate us from the love of God in Christ Jesus, 'neither death nor life, neither angels nor demons, neither the present nor the future, nor any powers, neither height nor depth, nor anything else in all creation' (vv 38-39).

In other words, God will get us there by his mighty sovereign power. He works in everything—in pain, in pleasure, in success and in suffering—to achieve the goal of making us like Jesus.

Some people worship a 'powerful' God who is limited to only some spheres of operation. This 'God' can send health, but not sickness. He can send prosperity and success, but not poverty and disaster. He can do the 'miraculous', but is somehow unconcerned with the small and ordinary things of life.

But hear what God, the creator and ruler of the universe says: 'I form the light and create darkness; I bring prosperity and create disaster; I, the LORD, do all these things' (Isa 45:7). This is the cosmic ruler who hears the sparrow fall and monitors the hairs on our head. He works in all things, not just in some things. There is no limit to God's involvement in our lives.

We should note one important consequence of this. If God is sovereign in the way we have outlined, then it is impossible to be 'outside the will of God' as some people use that phrase. Even our bad decisions are used by God to accomplish his ends.

Destined for Good Works

To fill out the picture further, we could look at Ephesians 2:8-10. It speaks more of our current journey than the destination:

> For it is by grace you have been saved, through faith—and this not from yourselves, it is the gift

> of God—not by works, so that no-one can boast.
> For we are God's workmanship, created in Christ
> Jesus to do good works, which God prepared in
> advance for us to do.
>
> Ephesians 2:8-10

We are saved *now*—saved from transgressions and
sins (v 1); from being an object of God's anger (v 3).
And we are saved wholly and completely by God,
so that we have nothing to boast about. It is his gift.
We are called 'God's workmanship', because he
has taken something that was dead and destined
for destruction, and made it into something en-
tirely alive, something that is worthy to sit with
Christ in the heavenly places (cf. Tit 2:14).

Note the purpose for which this new creation
has taken place—so that we might walk in the
good works that God has prepared for us to do.
Doing good works is not optional for Christians. It
is the very purpose for which we have been created. God has a way of living designed for us, and
he creates us (or re-creates us) to live that lifestyle.

Is any of this relevant?

By now, you may be thinking: 'Well, so far it all
sounds very "Christian" and right and true, I sup-
pose. But what has it got to do with me and my
decisions? How will all this help me to decide
whether to be a missionary or whom to marry?
When do we get to the guidance?'

Be patient. Many of our problems with guidance (and other things) arise because our thinking is distorted. We are very concerned about getting answers to *our* questions—today's questions—and we want today's answers. But very often, God's answer is: 'You are asking the wrong question. You are coming at it from the wrong angle altogether. You need to see things from my perspective if you want to live my way.'

The material in the last two chapters (and in the next three) is vital to the radical conclusions we will draw later in the book. If you do not understand or agree with what we have said so far, you will not accept the answers later on. Stick with it. You may discover that what you thought was so 'relevant' and important to your life is in fact quite trivial; and that the things you barely give a moment's thought to are the most important decisions you will ever make.

The passages we have looked at in this chapter teach us important things about *where* God is guiding us. They all teach (in different ways) the same basic message: that, just as with Moses in the Exodus, God is taking his people to the Promised Land, to heaven, to be submitted finally and completely to Christ, perfect and holy and blameless before him. There are many other passages we could have looked at to establish the same point. You may like to consult, for example, 2 Corinthians 3:18; Philippians 3:10-11, 19-20; Colossians 3:1-3; 1 Thessalonians 1:9-10; 5:9-11; 2

Thessalonians 2:13-14; 1 Peter 3:8-13; 2 Peter 3:8-13; 1 John 3:1-3.

We have seen that God does it all. He sets the destination, and he makes sure we get there! 'He who began a good work in you will carry it on to completion until the day of Christ Jesus' (Phil 1:6).

Does that mean that we do nothing? Are the things we do each day meaningless? Are our choices irrelevant?

The Bible is also emphatic about our responsibility to 'work out our salvation with fear and trembling' (Phil 2:12-13). Paul was under no illusions about the need for hard work:

> Not that I have already obtained all this, or have already been made perfect, but I press on to take hold of that for which Christ Jesus took hold of me. Brothers, I do not consider myself yet to have taken hold of it. But one thing I do: Forgetting what is behind and straining toward what is ahead, I press on toward the goal to win the prize for which God has called me heavenward in Christ Jesus.
>
> Philippians 3:13-14

The Bible urges us to respond to what God has done (and is doing) to achieve his plan. It warns us that those in the Exodus who did not obey God died in the desert without reaching their goal (see 1 Cor 10:1-13).

What response is required of us? What part do we have to play in God's guidance of us?

There is a right way to respond to God's plans

and his guidance, and there is a wrong way; and there are some classic misunderstandings. These three kinds of responses will be the subject of our next three chapters.

4

Right Responses

When the New Testament preachers called on their hearers to respond, what did they ask them to do? We need to take careful note of the answer to this question, for it will tell us how *we* need to respond to God's plans.

Typically, the required response was twofold, and Paul summarises it in these words: 'I have declared to both Jews and Greeks that they must turn to God in repentance and have faith in our Lord Jesus' (Acts 20:21).

Repentance = Turning

Repentance is about changing your mind, or more precisely changing your direction. 'I used to live this way, but now I have changed my mind and in future I will live this other way.'

Repentance means far more than feeling sorry. Sometimes it is associated with sorrow, but sometimes it is not (see 2 Cor 7:8f.). It is possible to feel very sorry about something but still keep on doing it—that is not repentance. It is equally possible to have a complete change of mind and action about something without feeling very sorry at all.

A good example of repentance is found in 1 Thessalonians 1:9-10. The Thessalonians used to worship idols, but after hearing the gospel they *turned* and began to serve the true and living God and to wait for his Son from heaven. Their change of mind altered their whole lives. They had an altered relationship with God, and an altered eternity.

This is just like the repentance that Jesus demands from his disciples. He calls on them to deny themselves, take up their crosses and follow him (Mark 8:34). Here is a radical repentance—to pronounce yourself dead and to start living for Christ. Paul puts it like this: 'He died for all, that those who live should no longer live for themselves, but for him who died for them and was raised again' (2 Cor 5:15).

By nature, we all live for ourselves. We do what we please (as much as others will allow us). We don't need to be taught this—it comes with our mother's milk. We know that it is anti-social and wrong to be selfish, yet we are all masters at it, and continue to practise it, to the detriment of ourselves and those around us.

A key part of the right response to God and his plans is choosing *not* to live for ourselves but for our Maker and Redeemer. In his death and resurrection, Jesus obliterates our past and opens up a new future for us. He makes possible a new start, a whole new life, in which we serve the living and true God rather than the dead and false god of our own Selfishness.

Faith = Trusting

The other key part of our response to God's guidance is 'faith', a misused and misunderstood religious word if ever there was one.

In modern Australia, faith means believing something to be true even though all the evidence is against you. Faith is a kind of blind, irrational leap (usually into the dark) in the face of all that is reasonable. This is reflected in the Concise Oxford Dictionary, which defines faith as 'belief in religious doctrines, especially such as effects character and conduct; spiritual apprehension of divine truth apart from proof'.

The Bible uses the word 'faith' to mean simply 'trust'. To have faith in someone is to trust them, or rely on them, or be confident that what they say is true. You may do this rationally on the basis of detailed evidence, or you may do it irrationally because your are gullible; but either way it qualifies as 'faith'.

As I write this, I am believing in a chair. I am having faith in it. My whole weight is placed upon it and I am trusting in it to do its job. It is not an irrational faith. I have been sitting on this chair for some part of most days during the last fifteen years, and it has yet to fail me. If I felt so inclined, I could examine the chair more closely to see if it was worthy of my trust. I could test its construction, analyse its design, and check all the joints. If it passed all the tests, I could then choose to sit on it, with my empirical rationality finally satisfied. However, I would still be putting *faith* in the chair (and, incidentally, in my empirical rationality).

Now faith understood in this sense (as trust or confidence) lies at the heart of our response to God. The gospel declares to us who Jesus is and what he has done. It tells of God's plans for the world and for each one of us, and it calls on us to turn from our present way of life (repent) and place our trust in Jesus (faith). Like the Thessalonians, we are to 'wait for God's Son from heaven'; that is, to put our 'faith' in him (1 Thess 1:10).

The New Testament makes much of this response of faith to the person and work of Jesus. In John's Gospel we read the famous words: 'For God so loved the world that he gave his one and only Son, that whoever *believes* in him should not perish but have eternal life' (John 3:16). Likewise, when the Philippian jailer asked Paul and Silas how he could be saved, they replied without hesitation: 'Believe in the Lord Jesus and you will be saved' (Acts 16:31). And writing to the Romans, Paul concludes (after a lengthy argument) that since 'we have been justified by faith, we have peace with God through our Lord Jesus Christ' (Rom 5:1).

Here then is the New Testament way of responding to God—we are to repent and believe in the Lord Jesus.

Is that all?

Is an initial response of repentance and faith all that is required? Our concern in this book is not just with our initial response to the gospel, but with our continuing response to God throughout our Christian lives.

When we examine this response more closely, we find that the continuing response to God is the same as the initial one. Repentance is something that we do once—decisively—when we hear the gospel and become Christians; and yet it is also something we continue to do throughout our lives.

Paul, for example, wanted the Colossians to 'put on' love; to keep clothing themselves in the characteristics and behaviour that befitted their new status as God's chosen people (Col 3:5-14). They had made a decisive repentance—there was no doubt about that. They had 'died with Christ' and had been 'raised with Christ' to a new life (2:20-3:4). Yet

Paul exhorted them to keep putting to death whatever belonged to their 'earthly nature'.   It didn't
stop with conversion.

Repentance is a continuing response to God.
The good works of Christian living are a natural
outworking of repentance.   Having turned our
backs on our old ways of life, we are now to walk in
a new way, following our new Master.

Likewise, faith is the ongoing response of God's
people to their Lord. God is our Shepherd, guiding
us towards home. The response of the sheep is to
trust. They hear the shepherd's voice and follow,
relying on him to get them home. Listen to what
Jesus said when the Jews asked him if he was the
Christ:

> I did tell you, but you did not believe. The
> miracles I do in my Father's name speak for me,
> but you do not believe because you are not my
> sheep. My sheep listen to my voice; I know them
> and they follow me. I give them eternal life and
> they shall never perish; no-one shall snatch them
> out of my hands.
>
> John 10:25-30

Jesus reassures his sheep that they will arrive at
their destination. And notice that Jesus equates
listening with following. We follow our Master by
listening to what he has to say and then doing it.
The Good Shepherd calls upon the sheep to trust
him, to follow him, to accept his guidance, to have
faith in him.

It is like a child learning to paddle a canoe. After all the instruction and coaching, there comes a time when the child has to paddle out by himself. This calls for trust in his father. He has to be confident that his dad will rescue him if he gets into difficulties. And he has to trust that his father's instructions about how to paddle the canoe have been correct. If he doubts his father's ability or willingness, then there is no point doing what he is told. If he decides to keep paddling his own way, then it is quite plain that he doesn't trust his father.

Our response to the Shepherd is just like this. We must be confident that he is both able and willing to fulfil his plans for us. If we possess this confidence, we will accept his directions for travelling on life's journey and obey them. The right response to God's guidance is to go forward confidently, knowing that God is at work in everything for our good.

Responding to God's Plan

Let's summarise.

So far, we have seen that God promises to guide us, and that this is what we would expect from what we know of his person and character and relationship with us (Chapter 2, 'O Thou Great Jehovah'). God's plan is to present us to himself pure and spotless in Christ on the Last Day, as he brings everything in heaven and on earth into

subjection to Christ (Chapter 3, 'Where to Moses?').
In response, we must stop travelling in our own
direction, turn around, and start going God's way.
We are to put our trust in him, knowing that he is
willing and able to get us to our destination. And
as we walk along the way, we are to continue to
repond to him by listening to his voice and obeying
him day by day (this chapter).

The basic response of God's people to their
Guide is repentance (turning) and faith (trusting).
We must have confidence in his ability and willingness to guide us and put that confidence into action
by doing it his way. The details of *how* we are to do
it his way come later in this book in parts 2 and 3.

Before we get there, we need to look briefly at
some classic misunderstandings and at how *not* to
respond to God's guidance.

5

Misunderstandings

It is a perversity of human nature that having the clear promises of God to guide us, we have such difficulty with the subject of guidance. Many have been paralysed with fear about missing 'God's perfect will' for their lives. Instead of being reassured by God's promise that he will care for us and bring us to our final destination, we live in anxiety. We are like children sitting in our canoes, desperately wishing to paddle ashore, and acknowledging our father's capacity to look after us, but terrified to take a stroke.

Let us look briefly at three common misunderstandings of how we should respond to God's guidance. Many of the difficulties people have with guidance are found here, in their failure to respond to God rightly.

False Repentance

In one sense, it is a dangerous thing to write about true repentance. It is possible to be too introspective, and to spend undue time worrying about whether we have *really* repented. This is unhealthy. Instead of actually repenting, we end up just analysing repentance. All the same, with this caution in mind we need to clarify the difference between real and false repentance.

The most common form of false repentance is to confuse repentance with feeling sorry. In a society as heavily dominated by feelings and emotions as ours, this is perhaps not surprising. Regret, disappointment, grief—these can all help give people the impression that they have repented. Yet, as we have already said, biblical repentance is changing your mind and behaviour.

Real repentance will show itself over time in a changed lifestyle. It involves turning away from our former way of life and leaving behind old patterns of sin. Real repentance will be seen in a desire to right the wrongs we have done, to make restitution. If we have changed our minds and committed ourselves to follow God's ways, then we will continue on the journey. We will undoubtedly sin from time to time, but we will keep travelling his way.

It is a little like marriage. At the beginning of a marriage, the partners make a decision that will affect their behaviour. They change their minds—

they decide to stop being single and to marry each other. This is usually expressed publicly at the wedding service, where they declare their intention to stop their old single way of life and start afresh as a married couple.

Having made this change of direction (repentance), the couple starts to act on it. They go on a honeymoon, buy furniture and set up home. They start to live as husband and wife. All kinds of emotions are involved in this process, before, during and after the wedding. Some of these emotions are extremely pleasant; others are not so great. But the emotions themselves are irrelevant to whether or not the couple is married. It would be a little strange if they came back from their honeymoon and then tried to analyse whether they were really married.

Repentance, like marriage, is a simple change of heart which results in a changed pattern of life. It can be over a small matter or over the whole way I live my life. It may be associated with emotions or it may not. But the only real indicator that the repentance is genuine is the changed behaviour that flows from it.

What if we should momentarily lapse? Many a husband has momentarily lapsed from his commitment to love his wife. However, that does not mean that he has ceased to be married. If his initial repentance was real, he will recommit himself to his promises and start again.

It is like learning new habits. Sometimes, the

old ways creep back in. The person who is committed to the new way of life will correct his error and continue in the new direction. The person who very soon stops correcting his errors and goes back to the old way of doing things is one whose repentance was superficial. It was not real.

What has all this to with guidance? Much in every way. There are many people who would like to identify themselves as Christians but who are not willing to forego their old manner of life. To some extent, we all carry with us vestiges of our pre-Christian past (sometimes very considerable vestiges!). But for many people, there is not even the willingness to change. They are satisfied with the emotional experience of having heard the gospel and felt sorry for their past; but they have no desire to turn around and lead a new life. There is no repentance (cf. 2 Cor 7 where two types of sorrow are contrasted: godly sorrow that leads to repentance and life, and worldly sorrow that leads only to death).

These people will receive no guidance from God. When he calls them to go a certain way, and they don't like it, they will refuse, or ignore it, or find some way of avoiding the issue. Guidance only comes to the humble—to those who sorrow over their sin, and are prepared to listen and change; that is, repent.

Faith in what?

Many people, Christians and non-Christians, misunderstand faith. Let me reminisce a little to illustrate the point.

School days were hard for me. I became a Christian in early high school and, in blissful ignorance and youthful zeal, set about tilting at every windmill I could find. I was frequently found without answers to the questions I encountered. Just as frequently, people were alienated from me and the gospel. Two of my most memorable traumas revolved around the subject of faith.

Once, when I was arguing with a teacher about the morality of his actions (there is no hide like a young hide), he turned on me with tears in his eyes and said: 'Jensen, it's all right for you. I would love to have your faith.' I didn't know what to do or say. I just stood there feeling stupid and confused and sorry and very embarrassed. I am still sorry I had no words to help that man.

On another occasion, I was explaining the gospel to a friend and he said: 'I want to believe. I've tried to get faith—I've really sought for it. But I just don't seem to be able to get it.' Again, I was stunned into silence. I knew how to deal with opposition (I thought). I knew how to cope with indifference. But what do you say to someone who wants faith but can't find it?

On both occasions, I didn't understand what faith meant in the biblical sense. Neither did my teacher or my friend. We all looked on faith as a commodity; as something you had (or hadn't). I was lucky enough to have found it. My teacher and my friend were still looking.

It is a common mistake. Many people think that faith is an object in itself.

However, as we saw in the last chapter, biblical faith is trusting in someone or something. We all have faith. We all put our trust in many different things, from the chair we are sitting on to the bus driver into whose hands we commit our lives.

Christians trust that Jesus did rise from the dead and live their lives based on that trust. Non-Christians equally trust that Jesus did not rise from the dead. They live their lives based on belief or confidence in that assumption.

In other words, it is not our faith (trust) that is important. It is the *object* of our faith that matters. If only my teacher and friend had known it. They had faith already, but they were placing their faith in the wrong object. If only I had known it, I could have been more helpful.

As we have already seen, the object of the Christian's faith is God himself—God the Creator and Shepherd of his people. We are to trust Jesus as our Saviour and mediator. We are to trust the words of God as true and powerful and active. We are to trust God's character and his attitude towards us. We are to trust his promises.

This trust is based on knowledge—knowledge of all God is, and what he has done and what he plans to do. God reveals himself to us in creation (Ps 19:1-14), through his prophets and ultimately through his Son (Heb 1:1-2). Only by hearing this revelation can we have a basis for trusting him (Rom 10:14). We would never have guessed or worked out God's great plan for summing up all things under Christ (1 Cor 2:6-10; Eph 1:8-10). It had to be revealed to us. And having had it revealed, we must place our faith (trust) in the revealed God, not in some god of our own making.

Active Faith

In Chapter 3, we looked at God's magnificent plan for the world and for our lives. We saw that in all of it, God was the sole agent, bringing his plan to completion in our lives in his own uniquely sovereign way. As Paul put it: 'The One who called you is faithful and he will do it' (1 Thess 5:23-24).

What response is appropriate to this? Based on what we have said so far, we might answer 'faith'? But what sort of faith? If God is so completely in control, do we really need to do anything at all? As a famous Christian expression puts it, should we 'let go and let God'?

Today, many people use the word 'faith' in this do-nothing sense. Several couples I have spoken to before marriage have told me that they planned not to use contraceptives because they were 'just going to trust God'. Similarly, some missionary societies call themselves 'faith missions' because they make no organised, human attempt to raise money: 'We just look to the Lord to supply the money.'

This is how many people today use the word 'faith', and we cannot say that God won't bless people who live this way. God, in his mercy, may give the non-contraceptive couple the two children they were hoping for (and no more). God is able to control the reproductive process—just look what he achieved with Abraham and Sarah! In the same way, God can finance a missionary society without the normal fund-raising efforts. The people of Israel did not leave Egypt empty-handed. God provided them with plunder from the terrified Egyptians (Exod 3:21-22; 11:2-3; 12:35-36).

But if we want to use the word 'faith' in its biblical sense, then we must not equate it with doing nothing. In some circumstances, doing nothing may signify a great trust in God; in other circumstances, it may signify unbelief of the worst kind. For faith in the Bible is an active reliance on God such that we choose to live his way. Having faith in God means taking action as he directs. If he directs us not to organise our missionary finances, then doing nothing is indeed the response of faith. But if he does direct us to organise ourselves, then doing nothing is *lack of faith*.

It is just this confusion that James addresses in the second chapter of his letter. Faith without works is dead, says James. It is not faith at all. Real trust in God will always result in good works, actions, deeds. Real faith will listen to what God says, accept it as the truth, and seek to put it into practice. Deeds are not the opposite of faith; *disobedience* is the opposite of faith. (A careful reading of Hebrews 3-4 brings this distinction out very clearly.)

Some may raise other parts of Scripture such as this:

> In repentance and rest is your salvation,
> in quietness and trust is your strength,
> but you would have none of it.
> You said, 'We will ride off on swift horses.'
> Therefore you will flee!
>
> Isaiah 30:15-16

However, when we look at such passages in context, we see that trusting God in that situation meant doing nothing because *God had told his people to do nothing*. This is quite different from saying that faith always means doing nothing and waiting for God. (We will return to Isaiah 30 later, for it is a great illustration of God's guidance of his people.) God does not get angry with people because they take action. He gets angry with them for taking their own action, rather than his.

In the Bible, 'faith' is not fatalistic. It is not sitting back and letting God do it all. Faith is an active relationship of trust and dependence and it is expressed in thousands of ways. If we trust God's power and love towards us, then we will pray to him for our needs and thank him for all that he gives us. We will listen to what he says and obey it. We will confidently follow his directions, knowing that they lead heavenward.

Such are the misunderstandings of how to respond to God's plans. Hopefully, seeing the misunderstandings has helped to clarify in your mind what the right response should be.

However, there are other responses to God's plans which are more than misunderstandings—they are just plain wrong. Many people reject God's guidance outright.

'Oh, I wouldn't do that,' I hear you say.

Wouldn't you? Read the next chapter and think again.

6

Wrong Responses

There are many ways to reject God's guidance. All of them are basically pagan in character, but sadly, many Christians practise them. For the sake of simplicity, we will group them under three headings: *Rejecting God's Power*, *Rejecting God's Generosity*, and *Rejecting God's Ways*.

Rejecting God's Power

Some reject God's power by using sophisticated intellectual arguments. Others resort to crude sinfulness. But the most common way is simply to ignore God—to treat him as if he didn't exist or as if he had no say in the affairs of the world.

We do this whenever we give up praying or

thanking him. We do it whenever we make plans
without consulting him, as if we were the sole
determiners of our lives. This is the exact reverse of
Jeremiah's prayer: 'I know, O Lord, that a man's life
is not his own: it is not for man to direct his steps'
(Jer 10:23). In the New Testament, James paints a
picture of the first century yuppie in similar terms:

> Now listen, you who say, 'Today or tomorrow we
> will go to this or that city, spend a year there, carry
> on business and make money.' Why, you do not
> even know what will happen tomorrow. What is
> your life? You are a mist that appears for a little
> while and then vanishes. Instead, you ought to
> say, 'If it is the Lord's will, we will live and do this
> or that.' As it is, you boast and brag. All such
> boasting is evil.
>
> James 4:13-16

People still live like that today; Christians among
them. They take no account of God in their plans.
They just make up their minds and do it, without
considering that the Lord of the Universe might
have something to say. Take the modern business-
man. He accumulates capital, runs a profitable
enterprise, makes wise investment decisions, and
through hard work gets himself into a position of
material and financial security. But just when the
final elements of his business plans are falling into
place, God visits him and says: 'You fool! This very
night your life will be demanded of you and then
who will get what you have prepared for yourself?'
Do you recognise Jesus' parable? (See Luke 13:13-
21.)

Making plans without God is a faithless course of action, but it is an easy trap to fall into, especially for those of us who are 'competent'. 'Phew,' you might think. 'I'm not at all competent, so that let's me off the hook.' But be careful. If you have ever succeeded in doing anything on your own, you are in danger of thinking that you can run other parts of your life too. We are very good at forgetting God and doing things our own way.

We forget that God overrules in all things, including our decisions. Consciously or unconsciously, we elevate our own decision-making above the power of God. We deny that God has power to influence and determine our decisions.

As we have seen in earlier chapters, God is in control of all things. He can take an action that was wrong and intended to do harm, and achieve his own good purpose through it. The story of Joseph is a good example. His brothers did an evil thing in selling Joseph into slavery, but God 'intended it for good, to accomplish what is now being done: the saving of many' (Gen 50:19-20). The cross of Jesus is the supreme example of this (see 1 Cor 2:7-8; Acts 2:23; 4:27-28).

God overrules everything—including the hearts and minds of people—to achieve his purposes. We reject God's power (and his guidance) when we act as if this were not true.

There is a strange heresy that has grown out of this rejection of God's power. It is known as God's 'second best'. Some Christians are taught that if God wants them to follow a particular course of action (marry Druscilla or serve on the mission field of Bolivia) and they choose not to do it, then they are committed for the rest of their lives to God's 'second best'. God had something better for them, but they missed out on it and so are required to settle for Plan B, so to speak. Many Christians today live in resentment, disappointment and guilt, believing that they have irrevocably missed out on God's perfect plan for them.

This view is a travesty of the biblical understanding of God. It contains numerous errors.

Firstly, there is a misunderstanding of sin and its consequences. The 'second best' theory seems to assume that there are only relatively few decisions that might place us outside God's will. However, our wrong decisions are not limited to a few areas (like marriage and career). We choose to rebel against God in hundreds and thousands of ways throughout our lives. Does each of these mistakes take us further and further away from the perfect plan? By the end of our lives, are we somewhere up around the '10,000th best'?

Closely related to the first error, is the very selective nature of the decisions that can consign us to the 'second best'. Things like marriage, career, answering the call to the mission field, and so on, seem to be viewed as very important matters of guidance, while the thousands of other decisions we make each week are somehow unimportant. As we shall see in a later chapter, this perception is false. The things we think are very important are often quite unimportant to God—and vice versa.

Most importantly, the 'second best' heresy denies the power of God. According to this view, once I have chosen my course of action, God is powerless to redeem the situation. He cannot rewrite the script. In fact, he is no longer a God with plans; he is a God with hopes. He is unable to achieve his goals without my indispensable cooperation, and is dependent on me making the right choices. He becomes subject to the whims and follies of human sinfulness.

Needless to say, this view of God is at complete variance with the way God is revealed in the Scriptures. As we have already seen, God overrules the minds and hearts of people to achieve his plans. He uses even our sinful decisions to bring about his purposes. We have already mentioned Jesus' death and the story of Joseph as examples of God using the evil actions of men to bring about his good purposes. These are not isolated instances. The Bible is full of examples of God working in and through people's minds and hearts. Here, briefly, are a few more examples for you to look up for yourself and think about:

- Notice how God hardened the heart of Pharaoh (Exod 7:3) and yet Pharaoh is also said to have hardened his own heart (Exod 8:15).
- Consider the range of influences bearing

upon Titus' decision to go to Corinth: 'I thank God, who put into the heart of Titus the same concern I have for you. For Titus not only welcomed our appeal, but he is coming to you with much enthusiasm and on his own initiative' (2 Cor 8:16-17). Titus is going on his own initiative and in response to Paul's appeal and because God put it into his heart!

- God's sovereign control over our minds is seen nowhere more clearly than in our conversion. For without God's intervention, our minds are 'hostile to God' (Rom 8:6-8). We cannot see the truth because the god of this age has blinded us (2 Cor 4:3-4). God, in his mighty power and love, opens our hearts to respond to the message; he opens our eyes to see the truth (see Acts 13:48; 16:14; 2 Cor 4:6). Jesus states it quite clearly: 'All that the Father gives me will come to me, and whoever comes to me I will never drive away' (John 6:37), and 'no-one can come to me unless the Father who sent me draws him, and I will raise him up at the last day' (John 6:44).

God's power stretches over all things, even over our wilful and sinful decisions. He may, and indeed does, call us into conscious cooperation with him in his plans. As we have seen in Chapter 4, 'Right Responses', he does demand a response from us. However, we must not think that the

accomplishment of his plans is somehow dependent on our participation, as if he were limited by
our freedom. The 'second best' heresy makes this
mistake. It is a classic instance of what is a distress-
ingly widespread problem amongst Christians—
the rejection of God's power.

Rejecting God's Generosity

The second way of rejecting God's guidance is as
old as Adam and Eve. In Genesis 3, the serpent
tempted Eve to distrust God's motives. 'You will
not surely die,' said the serpent. 'For God knows
that when you eat of it your eyes will be opened,
and you will be like God knowing good and evil.'
The serpent persuaded Eve that God was not acting
in her best interests; that his instructions were not
really for *her* good but for his own selfish purposes.

This denial that God is working for our good is
widespread in our society, and even amongst
Christians. We are constantly tempted to believe
that God is mean towards us, and that his instructions are specially designed to minimise our enjoyment of life. The world still tells us what the
serpent told Eve: 'Life would be much better if
you just relaxed. Don't get so hung up about
morality and sticking to your principles. Enjoy
yourself! Really, things would be very much better if you followed your heart and did what you
felt like doing, rather than following some out-

moded code of behaviour bound in a black-leather Bible.'

Christians are often portrayed as boring do-gooders or killjoys. This is a terrible caricature, and as false as the lie that the serpent foisted on Eve.

The best way to live *is* God's way. His commands are not burdensome (1 John 5:3); they are made for us to enjoy life. God made the world. He is the only person qualified to write the *User's Manual*. And because he is loving and generous, his instructions will always lead to the best and happiest life.

The whole situation is quite ironic. The non-Christian world likes to portray Christians as being trapped in a web of conformity, false morality and unhappiness, leading drab, pleasureless lives in the hope that somehow God will be impressed. The truth is that unhappiness is caused by *sin*, not by following God's ways. Sin destroys happiness; it destroys relationships; it deprives us of our freedom. The non-Christian world, enslaved as it is to sin, is full of broken lives and unhappiness.

Christians need to develop a healthy cynicism for the values of our pagan society. We need to laugh at the preposterous advertisements that tell us that Coke adds life, and that if only we used this particular brand of deodorant, our social lives would fall into place. Sometimes we envy the 'beautiful people' that populate TV-land. We look at what we have in Christ and feel a little cheated. Oh, that we would discern the immeasurable riches that are ours in Christ; that we would thank God for his incredible generosity to us; that we would have the spiritual wisdom and understanding to know what is best and reject what is false. Such are the prayer points of the apostle Paul (see Eph 1:17-19; Col 1:12; Phil 1:10).

The idea is conveyed elsewhere in Scripture. In Psalm 37, we are warned: 'Do not fret because of evil men or be envious of those who do wrong; because like the grass they soon wither, like green plants they will soon die away' (Ps 37:1-2).

There is also a positive promise in this psalm: 'Delight yourselves in the LORD, and he will give you the desires of your heart' (Ps 37:4). This is a fantastic promise of God's guidance for our good. The desires of our heart will be given to us. But what will they be? A Rolls Royce? A wife? A husband? A good career? If these are our desires, then we cannot expect to receive them, because we have bombed out on the first half of the verse. We are not delighting in the LORD.

'Ah, I knew there was a catch,' comes the protest. 'God promises to give me whatever I want, so long as they're only "God"-type religious things. Big deal!'

This is a very pagan objection, but it is made by too many Christians. We overestimate our own ability to judge what is good, and we drastically underestimate God's ability and willingness to give us anything for our good. On the whole, we are very poor judges of what is good. However, as

we 'delight ourselves in God' and begin to think as
he thinks, we will appreciate just how much he has
given us, and how good it is.

The Scriptures affirm that God loves to give
good gifts to his children and that he 'richly provides us with everything for our enjoyment' (Matt
7:11; 1 Tim 6:17). We must not doubt God's generosity toward us. If we doubt God's generosity, then
we will not follow his guidance. We will go our
own way, convinced that it will lead to a happier
life. And the result is always disaster.

Rejecting God's Ways

The third way of rejecting God's guidance is the
most common of all amongst Christians, and the
most varied in its forms.

As we have already seen, God has a plan for his
people—he has chosen the destination and a path
for us to travel on. Yet many people find God's
ways unacceptable, in part or in whole. They still
want to get to the destination (heaven), but they
map out their own route, full of shortcuts that are
personally advantageous. They want God to save
them and bless them, but on their terms.

There are many examples of this in the Bible.
We will look at just two, one from the Old Testament and one from the New Testament.

In Isaiah 30, the Israelites were under threat.
The unstoppable Assyrian army had Jerusalem in

its sights. The Israelites decided that an alliance with Egypt would be the best course of action, since Egypt could supply them with that crucial piece of ancient military hardware: the horse. The army with the horses won the battle.

But this was not God's plan.

> Woe to the obstinate children, to those who carry out plans that are not mine, by forming an alliance but not by my Spirit, by heaping sin upon sin; they go down to Egypt without consulting me; who look for help to Pharaoh's protection, to Egypt's shade for refuge. But Pharaoh's protection will be to your shame...
>
> Isaiah 30:1-3

God's way for Israel was quite different:

> In repentance and rest is your salvation, in quietness and trust is your strength, but you would have none of it.
>
> Isaiah 30:15

The Israelites were threatened by disaster. God had told them to put their trust in him, to sit tight and to let him resolve the situation. On the face of it, this seemed like a pretty stupid idea! With the threat of annihilation imminent, the Israelites decided to reject God's way and go their own way. The result? Their own destruction.

In the New Testament, the Colossians are one of the best examples of rejecting God's ways. They were in danger of 'moving on' from their faith in

Jesus to something new. But Paul warns them:

> See to it that no-one takes you captive through
> hollow and deceptive philosophy, which depends
> on human tradition and the basic principles of this
> world rather than on Christ.
>
> Colossians 2:8

Paul directs them back to Christ and away from
these side-tracks:

> So then, just as you received Christ Jesus as Lord,
> continue to live in him, rooted and built up in him,
> strengthened in the faith as you were taught, and
> overflowing with thankfulness.
>
> Colossians 2:6-7

Today, many Christians are in a similar danger.
Like the Colossians, they are impressed by religi-
osity, by rules, by asceticism and mysticism, by
visions and angels, and by the cleverness of human
philosophies. They don't seem to appreciate the
riches that are theirs in Christ, and so they go off
after the latest religious fad. They do not grow in
Christ, rooted in him; they grow away from Christ,
barely holding onto him!

Often, Christians are interested in extravagant
forms of guidance. Someone once told me, 'I
really have to leave my husband because I have
had a word from God that I am to divorce him
and marry Jack. I've prayed about it and don't
have any doubts. I've had a real peace come over
me. I've had a warm tingling feeling. You think

I'm joking, but I've actually had it.'

No doubt she did have a warm tingling feeling, but I don't think it had much to do with God. His unchanging Word says that we are not to commit adultery. Why would he send a warm tingling feeling to tell someone to do the opposite?

The seriousness of rejecting God's ways in favour of our own cannot be overestimated. Sometimes, it stems from an ignorance of God's ways; more often, it is the result of seeking to justify our ungodly desires. And when it comes to finding a loophole in order to avoid God's ways, our ingenuity knows no bounds. We need to heed the warning of the Israelites and the Colossians—rejecting God's ways leads to disaster.

The Story So Far

This brings us to the end of Part One. Let us look back briefly over the ground we have covered.

We started by seeing that God promises to lead and guide his people, just as he led Israel through the desert. As the Sovereign Creator of the world, he has the power to do it; as our Shepherd, it is the way he relates to us; and as the Supreme Planner, he knows where he wants to take us.

As he led Moses, so God is leading his people to the Promised Land, to heaven, to be submitted finally and completely to Christ, and to be conformed to his image. God has set the destination and, in his great power and love, makes sure we get there. Along the way, he has good works for us to walk in and calls on us to respond to his leading.

Our response to the grand design of God's plan is twofold: we should turn from our old way of life and follow God's directions (repentance); and we should trust him, knowing that he is both willing and able to guide us to the destination (faith).

This twofold response is often misunderstood. Repentance is viewed by some people as little more than feeling sorry. Faith is seen as a mystical commodity that you either have or haven't; or else it is identified with sitting back and doing nothing.

Some people go further and reject God's guidance altogether. They reject his power, his generosity and his ways.

So far, then, we have looked at the grand design. We have thought about the character of the guiding God, his plans for us, and our response. We have yet to explore the means by which God guides us along the way. How does God guide us? What methods does he use? How do we hear his voice so that we can follow?

It is to this subject that we now turn in Part Two.

PART TWO
How Does God Guide?

7

How Does God Guide?

What do we mean by 'guide'?

Up till now, you may have noticed that we have been using the word 'guide' in two quite different senses.

On the one hand, we have seen that God guides his people 'behind the scenes'. In his sovereign, irresistible way, God works in all things to move his people along the path he has planned for them. He turns our hearts this way. He pushes us in that direction. He arranges circumstances so that this may happen to us. And so on.

This 'behind the scenes' guidance is only visible to us after the event, as we look back on what God has done in our lives. We know that God is moving and working in all things for our good, but the day-to-day details are not revealed to us in advance. We *do* know the destination, and we *do* know that he will get us there, but God guides and shepherds us on our journey in ways that we can only guess at.

However, God does not only guide us sovereignly behind the scenes. He also calls for our *conscious cooperation*. He gives us certain instructions and directions, and calls on us to follow. With 'conscious cooperation' guidance, we *do* know what God wants us to do in advance. God says to us, 'Go this way,' and it is our responsibility to either follow or disobey.

In the following pages, we need to bear in mind this distinction between 'behind the scenes' guidance and 'conscious cooperation' guidance.

How, then, does God guide us?

Given the intense interest that modern Christians have in the subject, the surprising thing is that the Bible says very little about how God guides his people, especially in the area of conscious cooperation. There have been countless books written about guidance, outlining countless ways to determine 'God's will for your life'. Yet, in the Bible, the subject hardly ever arises. Furthermore, when guidance does come up in the Bible, the answers are very different from popular Christian piety.

I would like to suggest four propositions about how God guides:

1. God, in his sovereignty, uses everything to

guide us 'behind the scenes'.
2. In many and varied ways, God *can* guide us with our conscious cooperation.
3. God does promise to guide us by his Spirit and Scripture.
4. God does not promise to use any other means to guide us other than his Spirit and Scripture.

1. God, in his sovereignty, uses everything to guide us 'behind the scenes'.

As we have already seen in Part One, God is at work in everything. He is sovereign. Nothing is too small for him, if the hairs on our head are numbered. Nothing is too evil, if the death of Jesus was part of his plan. Nothing is too difficult, if half-dead Abraham and Sarah could have children. Nothing is too great, if the kingdom of darkness has been overthrown and Jesus sits at the right hand of God.

God guides us along the path in ways which are quite beyond our understanding. He uses anything and everything to achieve his plans for us, even turning our hearts and minds to follow his course (Prov 16:9; 21:1).

Moreover, he doesn't need our conscious co-operation to do this. Nothing can thwart his plans.

We must never underestimate God's ability to guide us 'behind the scenes'.

2. In many and varied ways, God *can* guide us with our conscious cooperation.

As we have already said, God's guidance is not only of the 'behind the scenes' variety. He does tell us which way to go and calls on us to consciously hear and obey.

From the very beginning of the Bible, God talks to man, giving him instructions, directions, wisdom and knowledge. God speaks to man in the Garden, telling him what he can and cannot do, and even spelling out the consequences of doing the wrong thing.

This is safe ground. We all agree that God speaks to man, that he gives us guidance by talking to us. The real issue is this: *How* does God talk to us? Should I expect a still, small voice? An inner prompting? A dream? Writing on the wall?

Hebrews 1:1 is a key text in answering this question:

> In the past God spoke to our forefathers through the prophets at many times and in various ways...

God can use anything to speak to his people and offer them guidance. He has spoken at many times and in various ways. The Bible records an immense variety of ways that God has spoken to his people. Here a just a few examples:

- God spoke to Moses from out of the burning bush, and then provided him with a stick that turned into a snake and a hand with on-again-off-again leprosy to persuade the people to follow God (Exod 3-4).
- God led the people of Israel out of Egypt using a pillar of fire and a cloud of smoke (Exod 13:20-22).
- God communicated his will through the Old Testament prophets, such as Jonah's word to Nineveh, and Nathan's rebuke to King David (2 Sam 7).
- God spoke to King Belshazzar by writing directly on the wall (Dan 5).
- God spoke to various people in dreams (e.g., Pharaoh in Gen 41; Nebuchadnezzar in Dan 4).
- Angels conveyed God's word to various people at various times, usually giving them a great fright in the process (Gideon and Mary, to name but two).
- God guided the apostles in their choice of Matthias through the casting of lots (Acts 1:25-26).
- Paul was guided into a new mission field by a vision of a man of Macedonia (Acts 16:6-10).

The list could go on. God can speak to his people in any way he chooses and call on them to go his way.

It is here that we must make a crucial distinction. To set out how God *can* guide us (or how he has guided people in the past) does not tell us how God *does* guide today or how he *will* guide. This is worth repeating: to set out how God *can* guide does not tell us how God *will* guide in our daily lives.

I have never been to Egypt. I don't have a staff, let alone one that turns into a snake. My situation and Moses' situation are quite different. Even if I met a man with a snake-stick and a hand with optional leprosy, I would not expect him to lead me out of slavery in Egypt. God *did* guide his people in that way. And I have no doubt that God *could* guide his people again in that fashion if he should so choose. Yet I cannot draw the conclusion that God *will* guide me in the same way today.

If we look at all the various ways that God *has* guided his people in the past, we do not find many promises that he *will* guide in the same way in the future. All of the above illustrations occur in narrative sections of the Bible. They describe how God guided or spoke in a particular time and situation. They say nothing of how God promises to guide his people in other times and situations—such as ours.

Modern Bible readers often make the mistake of assuming that because God *has* acted in a certain way in the past, we should expect (or even demand) that he act in the same way today. People choose stories like Elijah's 'still, small voice' or Gideon's fleece, and expect that God will guide them in the same way today. This is a grave misunderstanding. It is not only quite selective in the stories it chooses (you won't find many proponents of wall-writing in modern guidance books), it also ignores the uniqueness of the biblical narratives and their place in God's overall scheme. Worst of all, this way of reading the Bible takes no account of the difference that Jesus makes.

Let us clarify our question. What we really want to ask is not 'How *can* God guide?' or 'How *has* God guided in the past?', but 'How does God *promise* to guide us now in the area of our conscious cooperation?'. Having clarified the question, the Bible's answer is not hard to see.

3. God does promise to guide us by his Spirit and Scripture.

The Old Testament looked forward to a time when God would send his Spirit on all his people:

> I will give you a new heart and put a new spirit in you; I will remove from you your heart of stone and give you a heart of flesh. And I will put my Spirit in you and move you to follow my decrees and be careful to keep my laws.
>
> Ezekiel 36:26-27

In the New Testament, this hope is fulfilled. Jesus, the risen Christ, pours out the Spirit on his people (Acts 2:33). The New Testament continually assumes that all Christians receive God's Spirit as a guarantee of their relationship with God (Rom 8:5-7; Gal 4:6; Eph 2:18). Genuine Christians, writes John in his first letter, need not be worried by divisive heretics who deny Christ, because the anointing of God's Spirit will teach us the truth (1 John 2:18-27).

However, before we say too much about the Spirit's role in our Christian lives, we should realise that it won't help us much in answering our question: 'How does God *promise* to guide us now in the area of our conscious cooperation?' For who is the Holy Spirit but God? To say that God guides us by his Spirit is to say that God guides us by God. It doesn't answer the real question.

How, then, does God the Spirit promise to guide us? The answer is simple: by the sword of the Spirit, the Scriptures (Eph 6:17). God speaks to us by his word. He tells, directs, encourages, advises, commands, informs, reveals and exhorts us to live his way. The Spirit takes this word and applies it to our hearts. He awakens a response in us and leads us to put it into practice. This may sound very dull and pedestrian, but God speaks to us in words, and these words have been written down, and we are supposed to read them and find out what God wants us to do! This is not very mystical or magical or spectacular, and it therefore lacks some fascination for unspiritual minds.

When we look at what the Bible says about itself, we find a consistent pattern of promises that God will continue to guide his people by his word. And all the books on guidance agree at this point. They all give a prominent place to the Bible as a means of guidance. This is hardly remarkable, for the evidence within the Scriptures is overwhelming.

Let us spend a few moments looking at some of these promises, because the conclusions we will draw from them go far beyond what is said in most books on guidance.

Psalm 119 is easy to remember because it is so distinctively long. This is a shame in some ways, because people rarely read it or preach on it as a unit. Yet as we read its 176 verses, we are struck by the consistent emphasis on the importance of God's word to guide us in life. The psalmist strayed from God and was afflicted. He has now turned back to God and looks to him for salvation. He finds delight in obeying God's word and observes that his enemies ignore God's word. He longs for God and for salvation and for further opportunities to obey God's word, which he cherishes so highly. Almost every verse refers in some way to God's word—many give general statements about guidance:

> Blessed are they whose ways are blameless,
> who walk according to the law of the LORD.

Blessed are they who keep his statutes
and seek him with all their heart.
They do nothing wrong;
they walk in his ways.

How can a young man keep his way pure?
By living according to your word.

Your statutes are my delight;
they are my counsellors.

I gain understanding from your precepts;
therefore I hate every wrong path.
Your word is a lamp to my feet
and a light for my path.

Great peace have they who love your law,
and nothing can make them stumble.

Psalm 119:1-3, 9, 24, 104-105, 165

The way to life, wisdom, light and righteousness is in keeping God's word. As another psalm puts it:

The ordinances of the Lord are sure
and altogether righteous.
They are more precious than gold,
than much pure gold;
they are sweeter than honey,
than honey from the comb.
By them is your servant warned;
in keeping them there is great reward.

Psalm 19:9b-11

In the New Testament, Paul directs Timothy to persevere diligently in his obedience to the gospel and his teaching of the Scriptures, because in so doing he will save both himself and his hearers (1 Tim 4:11-16). The word of God teaches, rebukes, corrects, and trains in righteousness. It is the tool which the man of God uses to thoroughly equip both himself and those he teaches (2 Tim 3:16-17).

How is God going to guide me? By talking to me. How do I hear him talking to me? By reading the Scriptures. Do they show me the way I should go? They most certainly do, for they teach me how God wants me to live. They rebuke me when I depart from the way. They correct me to show the way back. They train me in the right way to go. The word of God is there to guide me every step of the way.

This is not just another example of how God *can* guide us; it his description of how he *does* and *will* guide us. His word makes our pathway clear.

Of course, not everyone agrees with this view of God's word. There are at least three alternative views that are worth mentioning.

Some professing Christians are quite explicit about rejecting the Bible's authority. They certainly do not value it above precious gold. For them, the Bible is a weak and fallible attempt to describe how God has helped man in the past. We may learn some lessons from it, but they are lessons we might also learn elsewhere. Needless to say, this view is at complete variance with how the Bible speaks of itself. This is not how Jesus regarded the Scriptures.

There are others who do regard God's word as authoritative, but as only one authority among many. These people look to the Bible for guidance and teaching as to how we should live, but are prepared to accept other authorities as well (such as the teachings of the church, or the dictates of their rational minds, or spiritual experiences). These extra authorities end up ruling over the Bible—they decide which bits we ignore or override. The Bible is still seen as a lamp to our feet, but a fairly feeble lamp that needs help from other torches and spotlights.

But the third alternative view is perhaps the most common of all. In this way of thinking, the Bible as a good strong light which clearly shows the way to go, but for only part of the journey. According to this view, the Bible lights up part of our lives and tells us how to live, but other sections remain in the dark. The Bible is said to give us help in a general way, but not about certain decisions—like marriage and career choice. For these additional decisions, other forms of guidance become necessary: such as direct words from God, inner promptings, feelings of peace, the counsel of godly friends, laying out a fleece, and so on.

This third alternative view is so widespread among Christians today, that it is virtually taken for granted. It is common to hear Christians say things like: 'I'm waiting for the Lord's leading about that decision'—as if God has not already given them sufficient guidance and is about to send them some special word or indication. Many are surprised to learn that this approach is a fairly recent development in Christian history—and even more surprised to find that it is not at all how the Bible views guidance.

These three alternative views of the Bible do not do it justice. They claim to use the Bible as their guide, but they do not take it seriously. In the next chapter, we will look at this question in more detail, but first we must outline our fourth and final proposition.

4. God does not promise to use any other means to guide us other than his Spirit and Scripture.

It is always hard to prove a negative. Ask any atheist! Unless you know everything, you cannot be sure that something does not exist. It may exist outside the bounds of your knowledge.

It is a little difficult, then, for me prove to you that God does not promise to use any means to guide other than his Spirit and Scripture. It may be that there is a promise in Scripture that I have not yet found. I am happy to be corrected. However, at this stage of my understanding, I cannot find a promise of God to guide by any other method.

Of course, we must remember that we are talking about 'conscious cooperation' guidance. We know from our first proposition that God uses everything at this disposal to guide us 'behind the scenes'.

We must also remember our second proposition: 'In many and varied ways, God *can* guide us with our conscious cooperation.' If he should so choose, God could still send us dreams, write on the wall, or appear to us in a burning bush. But in terms of what we should expect or look for, and in terms of what God has promised to do, Scripture (in the hands of his Spirit) is the only method.

Let me make the point more firmly (if that is necessary) by pointing out that God warns *against* numerous alternative methods of guidance. Some are fairly obvious, such as witchcraft and the occult (see Deut 18:9-22), but others are more subtle.

Jesus warns against following the traditions of men rather than the Scriptures, or in addition to the Scriptures (Mark 7:6-13). Paul also warns about becoming captive to human traditions and philosophies. These can come in a very attractive package, with all the appearance of godliness and cleverness, and with visions and angels and all kinds of regulations. But, says Paul, we must cling to Christ alone and grow in him, and not follow these false guides and be led by them into bondage (Col 2:6-23).

We must be wary of false Christs, false teachers and false prophets; some of whom can even work signs and wonders to try to deceive God's people (Mark 13:22ff; 2 Cor 11:4-5, 13-15). Even angels and apostles are not to be heeded if they preach a false gospel (Gal 1:6-10). It is worth noting how Jesus commends the Ephesians in his letters to the seven churches:

> I know that you cannot tolerate wicked men, that you have tested those who claim to be apostles but are not, and have found them false...You hate the practices of the Nicolaitans, which I also hate.
>
> Revelation 2:2,6

In contrast, the churches of Pergamum and Thyatira are rebuked for their tolerance of false teachers and guides.

I may be mistaken, but I cannot find any promises of 'conscious cooperation' guidance other than by Scripture and the Spirit, and I can find innumerable warnings against alternative forms of guidance.

This leads us to our next question: If God only guides us by the Scriptures, what areas of our lives do the Scriptures cover? Will they tell me whom to marry or which car to buy? What questions will the Scriptures answer, and what should I do if they don't give me an answer?

8

What Matters Matter?

Not so long ago, I went to a conference with forty medical students. I commenced proceedings by asking this question: 'What are the important decisions that you will face in the next couple of years?' The answers were relatively predictable: marriage, which hospital to work in, what specialisation to follow, what to do with all the money they would earn, how to cope with moral dilemmas such as abortion and euthanasia, if and when to go to the mission field, and so on.

These sorts of decisions seem to preoccupy young Christians (and not-so-young Christians as well!), and this is reflected in the case studies in Part Three of this book (on church, work and marriage).

Christians want to find God's plan for them in

these important decisions, so they look to the Scriptures for guidance. However, the Bible doesn't seem to be of much help. It only seems to speak in a general sense. It doesn't help me to decide whether to be a mechanic or a brain surgeon, or whether to marry Druscilla or Mirabel.

The traditional approach to this problem has been to distinguish between God's general and special wills. God is said to have a general will, applicable to all mankind and revealed in the Bible, and also a special will for each one of us that is not found in the Bible. God's general will tells us, for instance, not to commit adultery and not to be 'unequally yoked', but in order to choose between Druscilla and Mirabel we have to discern his special will for us.

How do we discover God's special will? The proponents of this approach usually recommend a combination of various methods: consulting older Christians, praying, seeking God's peace, putting out a fleece*, waiting on God, looking for signs, hoping for open doors, etc.

I think this traditional approach is wide of the mark. It does not take the Bible and its sufficiency seriously. To explain why, let me get back to my

---

* The practice of 'putting out a fleece' is modelled on Gideon's actions in Judges 6. Like Gideon, it is suggested, Christians may set a test for God to determine which course of action to follow, e.g., 'If Druscilla rings up first, dear God, then I will know she is the one you want me to marry; but if Mirabel rings up first, then she is your choice.' Needless to say, the practice completely misunderstands Judges 6.

encounter with the medical students.

I asked them another question: 'What colour is the equator?' They refused to answer. I asked them again. They still wouldn't answer. In fact, they told me that they couldn't answer and that the question was stupid.

This would have been very frustrating for me had I been an honest seeker wanting to know the colour of the equator. What if I really thought that the equator was coloured? If my friends continued to stonewall, I would have to turn to other sources of information to find an answer.

The point is this: if we ask the wrong question, we either get the wrong answer or no answer at all. And if we get no answer, we are tempted to turn elsewhere to find an answer. Could it be that sometimes we don't get answers from the Bible because we ask the *wrong questions*? Many of our problems with guidance stem from precisely this: we ask the wrong questions. We flounder around in great anxiety trying to discover the colour of the equator.

How do we know if we are asking the wrong questions? From what we have seen in earlier chapters about the sufficiency of God's revealed word, it would seem simple. If the answer to our question is in the Bible, then it's a right question. If it is not in the Bible, then it's a wrong question, or perhaps more correctly, an irrelevant question.

You see, God does not have two plans, one general and one special. He has only one plan, and it is both general and special. He wants all people, and each of us individually, to be under Christ. As we have already seen, he has a plan for each Christian to make us like Jesus by guiding us along a path of good works until we reach perfection on that Last Day.

God has given us all we need to know to complete this journey. If something is important and we need to know it in order to fulfil God's plan, then it is there for us in the Bible:

> His divine power has given us everything we need for life and godliness through our knowledge of him who called us by his own glory and goodness.
>
> 1 Peter 1:3

> All Scripture is God-breathed and is useful for teaching, rebuking, correcting and training in righteousness, so that the man of God may be thoroughly equipped for every good work.
>
> 2 Timothy 3:16-17

God has not left us in the dark, or in the twilight. He has not left out anything that is important for us to know on our journey with him.

God's agenda and our agenda are often very different. I am terribly concerned about choosing between Druscilla and Mirabel. I think the success of my whole married life will depend on the right choice, and I agonise over it. However, God's priority is for me to be a godly husband, rather than to marry a particular girl. After all, that is his plan—to make me like Christ. That's what he's interested in. It's at the top of his agenda.

How, then, do we determine the value of the questions we ask? The Bible itself determines the value of the questions, because it reveals to us which questions God thinks are important. As long as we pursue *our* questions, we should not be surprised when we miss God's answers in the Bible.

Does this mean that God isn't interested in the smaller details of my life? Not at all. God's plan to make us like Christ is more detailed and intricate than most of us ever imagine. It concerns every aspect of life. Let's take a simple example—driving a car.

Most of the decisions I make while driving are so trivial that I am not aware of them. I just drive. What could the Bible possibly say about driving a car? A great deal, as it turns out.

First of all, we must love our neighbour as ourselves (Mark 12:31). That tells us a lot about driving. The Bible tells us to be loving and kind to others, even if they treat us badly. What if the bloke in front suddenly cuts in, causing us to swerve and brake hard and giving us a shot of adrenalin? And what if we come across him broken down a few kilometres down the road? God has some guidance for us; he says that we should love our enemies and do good to those who wrong us (Matt 6:43). The Christian should stop and help.

The Bible also says that we are to obey those in

authority over us (Rom 13:1f.). Therefore, we should obey our government's rules about how cars are to be driven, which side of the road to drive on, and at what speed. Even if there is no policeman watching, we should obey the rules because that's how God wants us to live.

Add to this our concern for the safety and comfort of our passengers, and the potential for developing patience and self-control, and we can see that there is a very biblical way to drive a car. God has lots of detailed guidance about driving.

Notice, again, how the guidance that the Bible gives reveals what God thinks is important. Where you drive to, what sort of car you have, what colour it is: these things don't really matter. The minute-by-minute decisions to be kind, patient, loving and self-controlled are of tremendous and eternal importance in God's eyes. It doesn't matter much *where* we live. One place is much the same as another. But *how* we live, what sort of neighbours we are, how we raise our families—these things are of burning significance to God. Likewise, which job we do is of little importance, but how we conduct ourselves at work is close to God's heart.

In other words, the Bible tells *what matters matter*. If it's not in the Bible, it doesn't matter.

Three kinds of decisions

The Bible gives us all the information we need to please God and live a godly life. One helpful way of using this information is to separate our daily decisions into three categories. There are:

a) Right/wrong decisions;
b) Wise/unwise decisions;
c) 'Who cares?' decisions.

Let's look briefly at each of them in turn.

a) Right/wrong decisions

This kind of decision is fairly straightforward. The Bible sees certain things as always right and others as always wrong. Simple as that. God's guidance, for example, is for us not to steal or commit adultery or deny Jesus.

Sometimes there are things which are right in one situation and wrong in another. Killing, for example, may sometimes be right (Exod 21:14-17) and sometimes be wrong (Exod 20:13), and God tells us how to distinguish between the two.

Often in life, we are faced with these right/wrong decisions, and as Christians we should obviously choose the right. However, we need to *know* what is right and wrong, and we need to be *willing* (under God's Spirit) to do what is right and accept the consequences. In order to know what is right and wrong we must be well acquainted with the Scriptures.

b) Wise/Unwise decisions

In one sense, we need wisdom to know the difference between right and wrong, but there are also decisions that are more a matter of wisdom than right/wrong. Sometimes we are faced with two options that are both 'right', and we still have to choose. Each course of action might conform to God's standards of right and wrong, and we would be perfectly in the right with either choice. However, sometimes a consideration of godly *wisdom* would lead us to one choice rather than another.

Marriage is an example of this is, in 1 Corinthians 7. Paul is careful not to impose celibacy on people as a matter of morality, of right and wrong. It is right to marry, and it is right to remain single and celibate. It is a choice between two 'rights'. So how do I choose? Paul gives some practical wisdom on the benefits of marriage and singleness. If you can't control your sexual appetites, then you're much better off married. That is the wise course for you. If you do have the gift of remaining single and staying sane, then that would be a wise thing for you, because so much can be achieved for the Lord by a single person.

Christians often get confused about right/wrong and wise/unwise decisions. If something is simply a matter of right/wrong, then there is no need to search for further guidance—we should do what the Bible says is right and flee from what is wrong. However, if a decision is a matter of *wisdom*, then we should seek the counsel of the Scriptures and make our choice, without feeling guilty that we might be making the 'wrong' choice. If it's not in the right/wrong category, then we can't make the 'wrong' choice. Choosing either course is perfectly right and pleasing to God.

Decisions about which suburb we live in, for example, are not in themselves questions of right and wrong. Our motivations for moving to one suburb rather than another might be wrong (e.g., status, pride, greed), but the suburb itself is a matter of indifference. Yet our decision may be influenced by biblical wisdom. We may move to a particular location in order to avoid being in debt, or to be closer to a biblical church, or to reach a particular community with the gospel, or to reduce travelling time to and from work and thus have more time with the family, or for a host of other reasons which reflect a wise, God-centred way of thinking.

Any of our decisions in life, from the things we buy, to the politicians we vote for, to the way we spend our leisure time, can be influenced by biblical wisdom.

This means that Christians will make different decisions according to their differing circumstances and perspectives. For godly motives, we may decide in one context, say, not to eat meat, and in another context, for equally godly motives, to get stuck into the T-bone (cf. 1 Cor 8-10; Rom 14). This is quite possible with wise/unwise decisions. One man, in the wisdom of God, will choose to marry Druscilla; and another, also in the wisdom of God, will opt for Mirabel.

At this point, some Christians baulk. It sounds as if too much responsibility is being landed back in our court. What if we make the 'wrong' choice and step outside God's will for our lives? This is a knee-jerk reaction from our old, habitual thinking. If both courses of action are 'right', then both courses represent God's will for us. And we can't step 'outside God's will'—his plans can never be thwarted (Job 42:2).

What if something is in this wise/unwise area and we make an unwise choice (that is, a choice that is right but just not terribly wise)? Will I have to suffer the consequences? Most likely, yes. God wants us to learn wisdom, and very few people learn wisdom if their folly is continually rewarded.

However, God does protect his people—we do not need to be anxious about it. He won't allow us to be lost because of our own folly or to be tempted beyond our strength (1 Cor 10:13). He will pick up the pieces and make sure that we survive and grow through the experience. If it is in our best interests to suffer the consequences of our folly, then we will, but if it isn't, then God will spare us. We can trust his generosity and power to do so.

c) 'Who cares?' decisions
For the sake of completeness, we should say that there are some decisions that are very trivial and not worth spending time over. They are not matters of right and wrong, nor does the wisdom of the Bible have anything to say about them; e.g, whether to buy plain or floral print toilet paper. In these sorts of cases, we should simply make up our minds and choose.

The Story So Far

Before we turn to some case studies, let's glance back over the ground we have covered so far.

In Part One, we looked at the Grand Design. We examined God's character, his plans to lead us to heaven, and how we should respond.

In Part Two, we looked in more detail at how God guides us to the destination. You will remember that there were four propositions:

1. God, in his sovereignty, uses everything to guide us 'behind the scenes'.
2. In many and varied ways, God *can* guide us with our conscious cooperation.
3. God does promise to guide us by his Spirit and Scripture.
4. God does not promise to use any other means to guide us other than his Spirit and Scripture.

God communicates his 'conscious cooperation' guidance to us through the Bible (in the hands of his Spirit). The Bible gives us all the guidance we need to live God's way, and he does not promise to guide us in any other way.

The Bible tells us what matters matter, and which things are unimportant. It reveals God's agenda, and answers all the questions we need ask about how to live, even down to the trivial details of life. It helps us see that there are some things which are matters of right and wrong, and others which are in the realm of wisdom, and others which are matters of complete indifference.

For those of you raised on the traditional approach to guidance—with its special wills and 'second bests' and fleeces and peaces—all this is no doubt quite radical. But it is also quite liberating.

We don't have to flounder around, tentatively making decisions, hoping that we are pleasing God and sticking to his plan. God's will is not something hidden that I have to unearth. It is all out in the open and written down in black and white. All the guidance we need is in the Instruction Manual, and if something is not in the Manual, then we needn't lose too much sleep over it—we can just make up our own minds.

Choosing may still be hard sometimes, because in our sinfulness we will not want to go God's way. Life will always be complex, and at times we will struggle to work out how to apply God's guidance from the Bible. However, we can face our journey with joy and confidence, because our Heavenly Father is watching over us every step of the way. With the hymn writer, we can pray:

> Guide me, O Thou great Jehovah,
> Pilgrim through this barren land;
> I am weak, but Thou art mighty,
> Hold me with Thy powerful hand.

PART THREE
Case Studies

9

Church

We've looked at the theory; now it's time to put it into practice. In the next three chapters, we will apply our principles of guidance to three areas: church, work and marriage.

In doing so, we must recognise that in some ways we are falling into one of errors we've warned about: asking the wrong questions. We have lots of questions about church, work and marriage, and we think that they are very important. But as we have seen, God is more interested in Christ, salvation and obedience. The things that *we* think are important are not necessarily what God thinks are important.

All the same, it is important to illustrate how the principles we have looked at so far apply to real life issues, and how we can approach the

Bible to find God's answers. We need to proceed
with caution. We need to be prepared to have our
cherished views and priorities turned upside-
down. With this in mind, let us proceed.

Safe but Confusing

Church is perhaps the least controversial of our
three topics, but it is by no means the least confusing. The variety of churches and denominations is
bewildering. There are Catholics and Reformed
and Charismatic and Pentecostal and Anglican and
Orthodox and Presbyterian and Baptist and who
knows how many others? Even within the denominations, there is considerable variety between different congregations. Who are the good guys?
Should we identify our denominations as
'churches'? What should church be? What should
happen in church? The range of opinion is vast.

In the midst of it all, we have our own decisions
to make. Which church should I attend? How
should I choose? What should I do at church?
What should be my priorities? Where should our
church be heading? Where is God leading us?

At some point, we have to make decisions
about some of these things, and the choices can
be difficult. When we move to a new area, it is
sometimes hard to find a good church. Should we
choose the one with the same brand name as the
church we have just left? Which is better: a dull,

boring church with solid teaching, or a lively, go-ahead church with shaky teaching?

So far, we've seen that God promises to guide us by his word, and since it is *his* word, it is both authoritative and powerful. Let's look at how his word guides us with regard to church.

What does 'church' mean?

The word 'church' is used in a number of different senses in modern English. It can refer to:

- a building ('Isn't this a beautiful old church?');
- a job or profession ('Did you hear that Martha's boy has gone into the church?');
- a Christian meeting or 'service' ('How was church this morning?');
- a denomination ('A spokesman for the Anglican Church said…');
- a particular congregation ('I've just become a member of our church').

In the Bible, the meaning of the word 'church' is simple. The word which is translated 'church' (the Greek word *ekklesia*) is a normal, everyday word for *gathering* or *assembly*. This is illustrated in Acts 19 with the riot at Ephesus. The unruly mob that tries to lynch Paul is twice described as an *ekklesia* (in v 32 and v 41—the NIV translates both as 'assembly'). In v 39, the city clerk quietens the crowd and insists that if there is any genuine charge against Paul, it must be heard in a proper legal 'assembly'. Again, the word is *ekklesia*.

The only other Greek word that is used for the Christian assembly ('church') is *sunagoge* in James 2:2—it is the word translated elsewhere as 'synagogue'. The New Testament church is very like the Jewish synagogue. It is a meeting or gathering of Christians. (For a more detailed discussion, see the New Bible Dictionary article on 'Church'.)*

Who Gathers Where?

In the Old Testament, the word 'church' does not occur very often. The focus of Israel's corporate life was the temple. However, one very significant exception occurs in Deuteronomy 9:10 and 10:4, where the gathering of Israel around Mt Sinai is described as 'the day of the church' (NIV 'the day of the assembly'). Israel 'churched' or 'assembled' around God to hear what he would say to them (also see Acts 7:38).

In the New Testament, Hebrews 12 takes up this image of Israel gathered around Sinai and transforms it into a picture of the church under the new covenant:

---

* *The New Bible Dictionary*, 2nd Edition (Leicester: Inter-Varsity Press, 1982)

> You have not come to a mountain that can be touched and that is burning with fire; to darkness, gloom and storm; to a trumpet blast…
> But you have come to Mount Zion, to the heavenly Jerusalem, the city of the living God. You have come to thousands upon thousands of angels in joyful assembly, to the church of the firstborn, whose names are written in heaven. You have come to God, the judge of all men, to the spirits of righteous men made perfect, to Jesus the mediator of a new covenant, and to the sprinkled blood that speaks a better word than the blood of Abel.
>
> Hebrews 12:18-23

Christians have come to a different mountain, but the same God. In becoming Christians, we have become citizens of Jerusalem, the heavenly city. We are enrolled in a heavenly assembly ('church'), gathered around God, along with all Christians from down the ages. There is one place where the entirety of God's people gathers—in heaven around his throne. And, says the writer to the Hebrews, we *have come* to that gathering. We are part of it now spiritually, even though we wait for it to be revealed physically on the Last Day. Faith is being 'sure of what we hope for and certain of what we do not see' (Heb 11:1). Like Abraham, we are waiting for the 'city that is to come' (11:10,16; 13:14).

Whenever Christians meet here on earth, we do so as members of this heavenly church. This is the church: gathered in heaven, and in different loca-

tions and times on earth. In the future, at the end
of the age, the reality of that heavenly gathering
will become plain to all people—when Jesus appears, and we with him (Col 3:1-4).

That is why the New Testament does not simply
import Old Testament words like 'temple', 'sacri-
fice', 'priest' and 'worship' into the New Testament
church. The church this side of Christ is an assembly of God's people, reflecting and expressing and
foreshadowing the heavenly gathering. If anything, it is modelled on the synagogue, rather than
the temple.

According to the Bible's usage, then, many of
our modern 'churches' are not churches at all.
Denominations (like the Anglican Church or the
Presbyterian Church) are not really 'churches'—
they are organisations made up of a number of
churches. The real churches are the local congregations or gatherings, where God's people 'assem-
ble'.

This is what we understand the Bible to teach
about church, although it must be said that it is not
the dominant view in Christian circles. You may
disagree with it. We hope, however, that you will
suspend judgment for the time being while we
pursue the implications of this view of church.

Where is God Guiding the Church?

The answer to this question is fairly obvious in light
of what we have already said about God's plans,

and about the church in heaven. The conclusion
we reached in Chapter 6 was that as with Moses in
the Exodus, God is taking his people to the Promised Land, to heaven, to be submitted finally and
completely to Christ, perfect and holy and blameless before him.

There is also another image used to describe
where God is leading the church:

> Husbands, love your wives, just as Christ loved
> the church and gave himself up for her to make
> her holy, cleansing her by the washing with water
> through the word, and to present her to himself as
> a radiant church, without spot or wrinkle or any
> other blemish.
>
> Ephesians 5:25-27

> I am jealous for you with a godly jealousy. I
> promised you to one husband, to Christ, so that I
> might present you as a pure virgin to him. But I
> am afraid that just as Eve was deceived by the
> serpent's cunning, your minds may somehow be
> led astray from your sincere and pure devotion to
> Christ.
>
> 2 Corinthians 11:2-3

> Then I heard what sounded like a great multi-
> tude, like the roar of rushing waters and like
> loud peals of thunder, shouting:
> 'Hallelujah! For the Lord God Almighty reigns.
> Let us rejoice and be glad and give him glory!
> For the wedding of the Lamb has come,
> and his bride has made herself ready.
> Fine linen, bright and clean,
> was given her to wear.'

(Fine linen stands for the righteous acts of the saints.)

Revelation 19:6-9

The church is Christ's bride, and she is being prepared for her wedding day by pursuing righteousness. God leads the church to continue in Christ
and to grow, so that she will be presented 'pure
and spotless' on the Great Day.

What Should Happen in Church?

For guidance about what we should do in church,
let us turn again to Hebrews:

> Let us consider how we may spur one another on
> towards love and good deeds. Let us not give up
> meeting together, as some are in the habit of
> doing, but let us encourage one another—and all
> the more as you see the Day approaching.
>
> Hebrews 10:24-25

Christians gather to build one another up as the
day of Christ approaches. This side of heaven, we
are imperfect and much in need of each other's
fellowship. We need to be rebuked and corrected
and encouraged to persevere. This is what church
is for—to help us prepare for the 'wedding day'.
We gather in church to hear and obey God's word
together, so that we can be spurred on and encouraged.

In 1 Corinthians 12-14, Paul teaches much the same thing. He urges the Corinthians to allow the *edification principle* to determine what happens in their meetings. Whatever they do, it must be 'for the strengthening of the church' (14:26). The different gifts that God gives us must be used for the 'common good' (12:7). Paul uses the image of the body—a single unit made up of many different parts (12:12-26). Each part is important and should do its bit towards ensuring the health of the whole. In other words, love should direct what we do in church (13:1-13). We should only do what is helpful and 'edifying' for the other members (also see Eph 4:1-16).

The Importance of Church

In 1 Corinthians 3:5-17, Paul uses some slightly different images to describe church. He first of all likens the Corinthian church to a field, in which different workers have laboured under God's sovereign hand (3:5-8). The Corinthian church is also compared to a building that is slowly being erected—Paul laid the foundation (by initially preaching the gospel to the them) and now others are building on it (3:10-11). But they should make sure that they build carefully, because on the Day when we all stand before God, our work will be shown for what it is. It will survive only if it is quality work (3:12-15).

Continuing his image of the church being like a building, Paul describes the Corinthian church as God's temple (3:16). God's Spirit lives within the congregation, and this has a sobering consequence: 'If anyone destroys God's temple, God will destroy him; for God's temple is sacred and you are that temple' (3:17).

Going to church is a dangerous business. It is not something to be taken lightly, because we are not meeting with just any old group of people. We are meeting with God's temple. And God is vitally concerned about what we do when we're together. If, through our lack of love and ungodliness, we harm or destroy the congregation, we will have to answer to God. We should make sure that we only build with quality materials, materials that will last into eternity.

The importance of church springs from the plans of God. We tend to be very individualistic about Christianity—we often concentrate on individuals being saved. However, we must keep reminding ourselves that God's plan is to call *a people* to himself. The church is at the centre of God's plans:

> And God placed all things under his [Christ's] feet and appointed him to be head over everything for the church, which is his body, the fulness of him who fills everything in every way.
>
> Ephesians 1:22

Decisions About Church

Let us return, then, to the various decisions we face about church. The most obvious is which church to go to. How should we choose a church?

1. *Which Church?*

We have already seen that the church is God's people gathered together. Churches are gatherings of Christians. The first criterion, then, for choosing a church must be that the people there are Christians. The same applies for any group with whom we may want to have fellowship—we can only have Christian fellowship with those who are part of God's family.

It may seem strange to suggest that there might be churches which are *not* Christian, but it is an unfortunate fact of life. There are many 'churches' which are not enrolled in the heavenly gathering. How can you tell if a church is Christian?

In the New Testament, there are a few places where the line is drawn, where some guidelines are laid down for discerning real Christians from counterfeits. These give us some basis for immediately ruling out some churches:

- *Justification by Faith.* In Galatians, Paul insists that we are saved by putting our trust in God, not by doing good works. In Galatians 1:1-10, he states in very strong language that this is a case of black and white, heaven and hell.

If someone should come preaching this different gospel, then 'let him be eternally condemned!' A church that does not actively preach this gospel is not a true Christian church—we cannot have fellowship there.

- *The Real Jesus.* At a number of places in the New Testament, having a right view of Jesus is specified as a black-and-white indication of one's spiritual state. In 1 Corinthians 12:1-3, we read that only by the Holy Spirit can someone confess Jesus as Lord. Also in 1 Corinthians, we discover that the basic message of Christianity, as preached by Paul and the other apostles, must contain the 'word of the cross' (that Christ died for our sins) and the great news that he rose again victorious from the grave (see 1 Cor 1, 2, 15).

  In 1 John 4, John draws the same kind of line: 'Every spirit that acknowledges that Jesus Christ has come in the flesh is from God, but every spirit that does not acknowledge Jesus is not from God.' The true Christian embraces a Jesus who is the Christ, the Lord of all, who was and is God, and who became man. If the church you are attending has less than this view of Jesus, then it is not a true Christian church.

- *The Apostles' Words.* In 1 John 4, the Apostle John goes on to say that the true Christian (as opposed to the one who is 'from the world') listens to 'us', that is, the apostles:

> We are from God, and whoever knows God listens to us; but whoever is not from God does not listen to us. This is how we recognise the Spirit of truth and the spirit of falsehood.
>
> 1 John 4:6

The true church sits under the authoritative words of the Bible—and not just in theory, but in practice. Most churches will say that they acknowledge the authority of the Scriptures. We need to assess whether this is lip-service or a heartfelt commitment.

It doesn't really matter what brand name a church has—whether it has Anglican or Presbyterian or Uniting on its front gate. If it does not teach and model its church life on these sorts of truths, then we will not encounter *Christian* fellowship there. If we find ourselves already in a church that fails the above tests, then we should leave.

Another important factor in choosing a church is this: *Am I being edified and can I edify others?* We need to be sensible and clear-headed about this. The purpose of church in this world (as we have seen above) is edification—'building up'. If we are not being built up, and are not able to build others up, then our church is hardly fulfilling its function. We may well be wasting our time.

To be edified, we need to receive regular, faithful teaching from the Scriptures and encouragement to obey them. Edifying others, in one sense,

sounds easy. Surely we can build our fellow believers up in any situation, regardless of what is
taught from the pulpit. However, if our good work
is undermined the very next week by what is
taught and practised by the other church members, then our efforts are largely being wasted. We
would do better to move to a church that did teach
faithfully, and take anyone with us who was willing to go.

Within these guidelines, it doesn't really matter
which church we attend.

2. *Lifestyle Choices*

The overriding importance of church—of gathering with God's people to build them up—should
affect our decision-making in other ways.

It should affect our weekly lifestyle. If our work
and social patterns are preventing us from actively participating in our congregation, then we
have made some wrong decisions. We have chosen
to relegate what God considers to be supremely
important (loving other Christians) to a position
well below what *we* consider important (success at
work, money, a busy social life, and so on). If we
are to give more than lip-service to the importance
of church, then we need to make some simple,
yet sometimes hard, decisions. At the most basic
level, if we go to church on Sunday mornings, we
may need to decide to get to bed at a decent hour
on Saturday night!

The impact of the church goes beyond our daily

lifestyle. It should affect where we choose to live and work. Most people make their basic living decisions in this order:

1. find a job;
2. find somewhere to live near the job;
3. find a church nearby.

If church is as important as we have been suggesting, perhaps the above order should be reversed:

1. find the right church;
2. find somewhere to live nearby;
3. find a job that allows us to live near the church.

Now, life is rarely that simple, and, as we have seen above, there may be a number of suitable churches from which to choose. However, the principle is important. If you find yourself moving into an area where there is *no* church which complies with New Testament guidelines, then you may need to question your priorities. What is so important that it is making you move out of the reach of a good church? Perhaps you are moving in order to plant a new church! Or perhaps some other factor is motivating you, like a better job or a higher standard of housing.

We could usefully summarise these decisions by fitting them into the right/wrong and wise/unwise categories we talked about in Chapter 8.

Some decisions about church are matters of

right and wrong:

- All Christians should seek to meet regularly with other Christians to build them up (see Heb 10:24-25); we should order our lifestyle so that we can do this.
- We should choose a church that is Christian; that is, that bears the marks of authentic New Testament Christianity.

These decisions flow fairly directly from New Testament teaching. However, within this framework, there are other decisions which are matters of wisdom:

- Within the pool of genuinely Christian churches, we should exercise wisdom in choosing which church to belong to. Since the purpose of church is mutual edification, we would be wise to choose a church in which we will be edified and in which we will have opportunity to edify others.
- The Bible's wisdom would also suggest that, since church is extremely important, we would do well to order our priorities so that we can be actively involved in our churches.

10
Work

I like work; it fascinates me. I can sit and look at it for hours. I love to keep it by me: the idea of getting rid of it nearly breaks my heart.

Jerome K Jerome, 'Three Men in a Boat'

Most of us have a love-hate relationship with work. We can't live without it—either physically or psychologically—and yet it is also a source of frustration, weariness, boredom and indecision. Work dominates our waking hours and so it is hardly surprising that it generates many, many decisions.

For those young enough and fortunate enough to have a choice about which job to take, the most pressing question may seem to be which career to follow. But there are many other questions as well:

- Is it important to have job satisfaction?
- What if my job is not fulfilling or enjoyable—am I expected to stick at this for the next twenty years?
- Is how much I earn important in choosing a job?
- What if I can't get a job?
- Should a Christian go on the dole?
- Should I enter the ministry or go to the mission field?
- How can I use my job to further the gospel?
- Should I accept promotion if it is going to mean less time for my family?
- Is it right to evangelise my clients and workmates during work time?

Looking for the Bible's Answers

In turning to the Bible, we must first lift our eyes off our own particular questions. We must remind ourselves that *our* perspective and *God's* perspective are very different—and his perspective is right! We have to be ready to hear God's answers to the questions *he* says are important.

We may find a particular Bible verse that speaks directly to our circumstances. If you are a converted thief, for example, you have your very own verse in Ephesians 4:28. However, for the most part, we will have to rely on applying general biblical wisdom and values to our situation.

What follows is a brief outline of the Bible's teaching about work. It is not an exhaustive study, and no doubt it could have been arranged differently. There are seven headings.

1. God in Creation

God, Genesis tells us, worked six days and rested one when he created the world. This may not strike you as odd (perhaps because our culture has been built on this pattern), but it is extremely significant. God is a worker. We do not worship a God of idleness and frivolity. God works and rests—and the two are kept quite separate. We will see how important this separation is below.

2. Mankind in Creation

God places mankind in the creation to rule and subdue it (Gen 1:26-28). Adam is to tend the garden and take care of it (Gen 2:15). He is given work to do as part of God's created order (cf. Ps 104:23).

The Bible assumes that mankind will have to work, just as we need to eat and drink and sleep. The Book of Proverbs condemns idleness and laziness, and encourages diligence and perseverance in our work (Prov 26:13-16; 28:19; 21:25-26; 20:4,13). Even Ecclesiastes, for all its worldly pessimism, speaks of man finding satisfaction in his toil (Eccles 3:13).

Moreover, work is not just the privilege of God's people; it extends to all creation. The ungodly line of Cain is noted for its work in building cities, raising livestock, playing music, and making tools of bronze and iron (Gen 4).

3. The Fall and Work

After the Fall, man's work is affected by God's judgment. Adam is told that work in the fallen world will be a struggle. The ground itself will be hostile to his efforts to subdue it (Gen 3:17-19). After Cain murders his brother, the ground is cursed again and Cain is forced to give up his farming and wander the earth (Gen 4:10-12).

There is some relief from this struggle in the story of Noah. God says that he will 'never again curse the ground...and never again will I destroy all living creatures as I have done' (Gen 8:21-22). However, the world remains disordered and fallen even after Noah. It is still subjected to futility and 'bondage to decay' (Rom 8:20-22).

The Fall also affects work indirectly. In a fallen, sinful world, work is just one more opportunity for us to express our sinfulness. In Genesis 11:1-10, we find mankind banding together to work for a common goal—the godless Tower of Babel. Throughout human history, work has been characterised by injustice, exploitation, immorality, cheating, greed and arrogance (e.g., Amos 8:4-6; Jas 4:13-14). Sinful man uses work as a means to achieve his own godless ends.

4. Human Work and God's Character

Just as God worked and rested, so the people of

Israel were commanded to work and rest (Exod
20:8-11). Israel's law made provision for the just
payment of all those who work (Lev 19:13), even
the ox (Deut 25:4). In the New Testament, we are
told that this was written for our sake so that we
would know how to treat those who work in
gospel ministry (1 Tim 5:18; 1 Cor 9:7-12 — see
point 6 below).

The Scriptures give clear instructions about
how we should work, especially in our relationships with our colleagues. Colossians 3:22-4:1 and
Ephesians 6:5-9 speak of how the relationship between slaves and masters should be modelled on
the relationship between Christ and his people.
We are exhorted to be diligent, honest, sincere, just
and generous. These sorts of values are also found
in John the Baptist's advice to tax collectors and
soldiers (Luke 3:12-14), and Paul's word to thieves
(Eph 4:28). We may have to do some thinking
about how the slave/master structure of the first
century relates to own employee/employer relationships, but the principles are fairly clear. God
wants us to work in a way that reflects his character and our relationship with him.

There is very little instruction about *what* work
we are to do, except that it cannot be inherently
dishonest or ungodly (e.g., the thief). However,
there is plenty of instruction about *how* we are to
work: with enthusiasm, honesty and fairness, serving the Lord in the tasks we do. God gives us a
general direction to rule and subdue the earth, but

beyond this, he gives us no career guidance.

This may not satisfy our desire to receive a divine stamp of approval for our particular profession. However, we cannot go beyond what God has said. He has said plenty about the manner in which we work. It obviously matters to him a great deal. It should also matter to us.

5. *Christian Motivations for Work*

There is no more important Bible passage in constructing a Christian view of work than 2 Thessalonians 3:6-14, because it deals directly with the subject. In this passage, Paul explains to the Thessalonians why they should be working. He also gives some indirect but very helpful teaching about the place and value of work in our Christian lives. The passage is worth reading in full:

> In the name of the Lord Jesus Christ, we command you, brothers, to keep away from every brother who is idle and does not live according to the teaching you received from us. For you yourselves know how you ought to follow our example. We were not idle when we were with you, nor did we eat anyone's food without paying for it. On the contrary, we worked night and day, labouring and toiling so that we would not be a burden to any of you. We did this, not because we do not have the right to such help, but in order to make ourselves a model for you to follow. For even when we were with you, we gave you this rule: 'If a man will not work, he shall not eat.' We hear that some among you are idle. They are

> not busy; they are busybodies. Such people we
> command and urge in the Lord Jesus Christ to
> settle down and earn the bread they eat. And as
> for you, brothers, never tire of doing what is right.

Paul musters all his apostolic authority to command the Thessalonians to follow his example and work for their bread. The reason for this is simple: everyone has to eat. If you don't earn your food yourself, you have to sponge off someone else. This is self-centred and unloving. Therefore, says Paul, stop being a burden on others and work for your food. If you're not prepared to work, then you shouldn't expect to eat. (The other reason Paul gives is that idlers tend to be busybodies.)

In other words, for Paul, working is simply a matter of survival. We work in order to eat and not be a burden on others (cf 1 Thess 4:11; Prov 16:26).

Another motivation for work is given in Ephesians 4:28, a verse we have already mentioned:

> He who has been stealing must steal no longer,
> but must work, doing something useful with his
> own hands, that he may have something to share
> with those in need.

The ex-thief is to do something useful with his hands (as opposed to what he used to do with his hands) so that he can give to those in need. Here is an additional motivation for work: it is not only to feed our faces, but also so that we have something to share with others. Notice how the thief has come full circle. He no longer takes—he gives. And by giving to the needy he removes from them the temptation to steal.

So far, we have avoided trying to give a hair-splitting definition of 'work'. Paul expects all Christians to work. Yet this must be read in light of his instruction regarding widows in 1 Timothy 5. The older godly widows are to be put on a pension, but the younger widows are directed back to work in much the same terms as the Thessalonians. The only difference is that 'work' for the younger widows is to marry, have children and manage their homes. The New Testament directs all Christians to work.

6. Gospel Preaching as an Alternative to Work
Within the New Testament, there is one exception to the rule about work—gospel preaching.

> 'Come, follow me,' Jesus said, 'and I will make you fishers of men.' At once they left their nets and followed him.
>
> Mark 1:17-18

When Jesus sent out the seventy, he told them to accept any food or drink they are given because 'the worker deserves his wages' (Luke 10:7). Paul picks up this phrase in his instructions to Timothy (1 Tim 5:17-18). Gospel work—the preaching and teaching of the good news of Jesus—is to be considered as work deserving of pay.

Paul himself chose to work with his hands at

various points in his ministry. Yet, he stoutly defends his right to stop manual labour and live off his ministry. He worked so as not to be a burden, to bring the gospel free of charge, and to set an example to the believers. However, he did not work in order to eat, nor because he was compelled (1 Cor 9:1-18; cf. Gal 6:6).

In other words, while the New Testament clearly teaches that all Christians should work, it also teaches that there is one group who need not work with their hands for their food—the preachers of the word of God. Their 'work' is specifically 'Christian' work, which only Christians can be expected to appreciate and support financially. Gospel preachers are God's fellow workers (1 Cor 3:9; 2 Cor 6:11), for they participate in God's ongoing work in the world—the proclamation of Christ for mankind's salvation.

7. *Work as an Alternative Gospel*
Not all Christians agree with what we have just said about gospel preaching being an alternative to work. There is a strong current of Christian opinion today that says that work itself can be an alternative form of gospel preaching.

It is argued that by working in the world and contributing to society, Christians can do as much (if not more) for the kingdom of God than by outright evangelism. People claim that their work as Christian doctors or lawyers or teachers gives glory to God and advances the cause of the gospel (interestingly, garbage collectors and street sweepers are rarely mentioned in this connection).

We have already said that it is right and godly to work for a living, and that the way we do our work can bring glory to God (e.g., by being honest and diligent). However, we must not confuse our obligation to work with the ministry of the gospel.

Those who put forward work as an alternative method of preaching the kingdom have not grasped how God works in the world. God's work of drawing people to himself is accomplished by the proclamation of Christ crucified. It happens when people who know the good news tell other people who don't.

We may do some of this proclamation while we are at work. Normal employment often provides marvellous opportunities for sharing the good news with people who might otherwise never come into contact with a Christian. However, we must be clear about it—it is not our work, as such, that is fulfilling God's plans for the world; it is our testimony to workmates and clients (i.e., our gospel preaching) that is being used by God in the work of his kingdom.

We fulfil God's plans (or will) when we work in a godly way. It doesn't really matter what job we do, so long as we do it in a way that honours God. The one exception is gospel preaching—this is a work that, in and of itself, fulfils God's plans for the world.   In other words, a civil engineer does not contribute to God's kingdom by the bridges he builds. These may be very worthwhile structures, and useful in society. However, they belong to this world only. The Sunday School teaching that the engineer does on Sunday is of a different order. It may not be very impressive, or prestigious, or even very satisfying, but it is part of God's work in the world.

Most of us do this gospel work part-time, as it were, squeezing it in around our other responsibilities. Others, because of their particular gifts, may be freed from earning their bread in order do 'the Lord's work' full-time.

Clearing the Ground

Before we apply this brief summary of the Bible's teaching on work to our daily decisions, it might be helpful to clear the ground of some confusing debris. Sometimes it is useful to make explicit what the Bible has *not* said, because many of the questions we raise are in areas where the Bible is pointedly silent.

1. *Status and Jobs*

It is almost axiomatic in the Western world that our job is an indicator of our status. We *are* what we *do*. It is certainly a common way to open a conversation. 'And what do you do?' we ask innocently, knowing that the person's answer will immediately tell us whether they are above us or below us on the social pecking order. This pecking order seems fairly well established. Surveys of which jobs are held in the highest esteem come out with fairly consistent results—judges and specialist doctors up the top, real estate agents and used car salesmen down the bottom.

We are so conditioned to look for significance and status through our employment that it is very hard for us to think otherwise. *These Ruins are Inhabited** is a delightful book about an American family's study leave in Oxford. The wife (and author of the book) has this unwittingly pathetic thing to say of her husband:

> I've done my husband an injustice. I've given the impression that he's an average American husband and father, cooler-tempered than some, warmer-hearted than others, an ex-Nebraska farm boy who has never outgrown an addiction to puns and who in Britain acquired an addiction to pre-historic relics. All that is true. But the most important fact about George is that he is a Scientist.

George's work, according to his wife, is the key to his character, his significance, his value. It is the single most important thing about him. Too bad if he was a parking attendant.

How does this compare with what the Bible says about work? As we have already seen, the

---

* *These Ruins Are Inhabited*, Beadle (Hale Publishers, 1989)

Bible is silent about *what* we do. Instead, it urges us to find our significance and value in being created by God, in being redeemed by his Son, in being the temple of his Holy Spirit. James puts it clearly in connection with wealth and poverty:

> The brother in humble circumstances ought to take pride in his high position. But the one who is rich should take pride in his low position, because he will pass away like a wild flower.
>
> James 1:9-10

Paul speaks in the same vein about our social standing:

> Each one should remain in the situation which he was in when God called him. Were you a slave when you were called? Don't let it trouble you— although if you can gain your freedom, do so. For he who was a slave when he was called by the Lord is the Lord's freedman; similarly, he who was a free man when he was called is Christ's slave. You were bought at a price; do not become slaves of men. Brothers, each man, as responsible to God, should remain in the situation God called him to.
>
> 1 Corinthians 7:20-24

Modern attitudes about the value and status of work are part of the baggage that we carry with us as Christians. If we are to make godly decisions about our work, we must first jettison this baggage. It will prevent us from seeing clearly what God wants us to do.

2. Job Satisfaction

There is a second confusion: that somehow our
jobs should be satisfying or fulfilling. The Christian is mercifully free from this—or at least we
should be—because of the fulfilment and satisfaction that we find in Christ. There are many Christians who have still not worked this one out, and
who labour under the delusion that they should
only accept a job that is 'fulfilling'.

The Bible says very little about job satisfaction,
other than to indicate that it is a blessing if you
have it (Eccles 3:13) and that we can expect work to
be difficult and frustrating (Gen 3:17-19).

It is not hard to see why the Bible says so little
about job satisfaction. Firstly, and most obviously,
our 'fulness' is to be found in Christ and nowhere
else (Col 2:6-12). Ecclesiastes concedes that it is a
great thing to be satisfied with one's toil, but the
overall message of the book is bleak—even if you
are blessed enough to derive some satisfaction
from your work, it is still all meaningless. Only in
God can we be satisfied. Only he gives water that
truly quenches our thirst (John 4:13-14).

Secondly, the Bible is addressed to the vast
majority of humankind for whom work is not a
pleasure but a necessity. Having a choice of jobs is
a luxury afforded to only a tiny fraction of the
world's population, both now and throughout
history.

Some time ago, I asked my father why he chose
to become a printer—printing being such a repeti-

tive and seemingly boring job, and my father being such an intelligent man. In a gentle way, he showed me what a stupid question it was. When he was a boy with a widowed mother and four siblings, before the days of government pensions and social welfare, he had very little choice about which job he would take. In his country town, several hundred boys applied for the two apprenticeships available that year. Although it meant leaving school at 12, he was the envy of the others when he landed one of the coveted apprenticeships. 'Choice of career' is a plaything of the rich.

Does this mean that I must take a boring, dissatisfying job? No, not at all. But it *does* mean that job satisfaction and lack of boredom are of little consequence in our Christian thinking about work. If your job is satisfying, then give praise to God. You are blessed, and not many are blessed in that way—make sure that your satisfying job does not replace Christ in your affections. If your job does not satisfy you, then labour on, and remember who your real Master is:

> Whatever you do, work at it with all your heart, as working for the Lord, not for men, since you know you will receive an inheritance from the Lord as a reward. It is the Lord Christ you are serving.
>
> Colossians 3:23-24

3. Work and Power

Another confusing factor in our thinking about work is power. Some jobs seem to drip with power. The politician, the doctor, the media commentator—these jobs seem to have great potential for both good and evil. They appear to alter the course of society. Some Christians think that by getting into these positions of power they will be able to do a great work for God.

Firstly, we must question how much good the 'powerful' people can really do. It is not as simple as it seems. The farmer who provides quantities of fresh food makes an enormous contribution to society. So does the engineer who constructs safe, hygienic sewerage systems. In fact, together they probably contribute more to public health and well-being than the entire medical profession. The 'powerful' people may not be as powerful as they like to maintain.

Secondly, we must remember that God has chosen only one way to change human society, and that is through the proclamation of Christ. It is the gospel which is God's power for salvation. Food and clothing may be God's gift to us, and it is a worthwhile job to provide them, but we must keep our eyes on the overriding priority of seeing people come to know God. Full bellies and warm clothes do not get people right with God.

The Christian, then, may well choose to work in occupations that serve some useful purpose in society. But we must never think that we are doing more than applying bandaids. Social work, medicine, politics, sewerage construction—none can replace gospel preaching.

4. The Place of Money

Christians are ambivalent about the money they get for working. Many feel that to choose one job over another because it pays more seems cheap and unworthy. Others are only too happy to choose the better paying job, and then fall in love with the material rewards it brings.

We should avoid both of these extremes. We shouldn't be the slightest bit embarrassed about earning lots of money for working. After all, the main reason given for working in 2 Thessalonians 3 is material return. By earning more, we can have more to share with others. We can give to those in need, and provide for the spread of the gospel. However, we will also have to take into account the costs involved in taking a highly paid job. More pay almost always means more time and/or responsibility. What effects will this have on my Christian life, on my family, on my involvement at church?

We should be especially careful to avoid the other extreme. Money is not evil, but the *love of money* is incompatible with serving God. You can't love both, so don't try. As Jesus said:

> No-one can serve two masters. Either he will hate .
> the one and love the other, or he will be devoted to
> the one and despise the other. You cannot serve
> both God and Money.
>
> Matthew 6:24

Applying the Bible Today

With the Bible's teaching summarised, and the
ground cleared of some of its more dangerous
obstacles, perhaps we can now make some decisions about work.

1. Work
In all normal circumstances, we should all seek to
be usefully and gainfully employed.

2. Rest
We must balance our work with rest. God wants us
to take a day off each week to be refreshed and to
remember all that he has done for us.

3. Godliness
Whatever job we do, we must conduct ourselves in
a manner worthy of our Lord: honestly, fairly,
whole-heartedly.   This will exclude some jobs
altogether and make others difficult.

4. Ambition
Our goals in life should revolve around God's
kingdom and his righteousness, not ourselves. The
way we work is therefore of far greater significance
than the particular job we take. Work is simply
what we do to earn our bread. It is not a 'career'
by which we hope to find fulfilment, satisfaction
or status.

5. *Gospel*

While values such as honesty and justice may affect which jobs we take and how we work, the gospel has a particularly important place in work decisions. The work of the gospel should be our first priority, and we should make our job decisions in light of this priority. In other words, 'Will my promotion affect the Sunday School class I'm teaching?' is an important and proper question to ask.

6. *Drawing Lots*

If you are faced with a choice between two virtually identical alternatives, then don't lose sleep over it. Either way, it will be all right. If you are really stuck, then drawing lots or tossing a coin is as good a method of Christian guidance as any other.

11

Marriage

The prevailing attitudes and values of our culture influence us in many ways, but never more profoundly than in relation to marriage and family. As we observe our parents' marriage and grow up in their family, we develop a strongly-held set of values about marriage and family life.

It is hard, perhaps impossible, to erase the legacy of our upbringing in this area. Our views are reinforced by others in our society—the friends we mix with at school, the traditions of our particular cultural background, and the steady stream of images pumped into us by the media.

This makes it difficult for us when we approach marriage as Christians. As we enter marriage, we carry with us a busload of expectations and entrenched attitudes, some of them below the level of consciousness.

And when we turn to the Bible for guidance about Christian marriage, we can be puzzled by the strange ideas that we encounter. The Bible has strong things to say about marriage, but they are radically different from the values of our culture.

As with our previous case studies, our first task is to take a quick look at what the Bible as a whole teaches us about our subject. Again, we must emphasise that this is a superficial summary of the Bible's teaching—a whole book could be written on each of the following topics.

The First Marriage

Much of the Bible's guidance on marriage stems from its opening chapters. From the very beginning, God made mankind for relationship. In Genesis 1, God makes Man in his image, and one facet of that image is that, like God, we are diverse and yet united, and enjoy relationship with each other. We are male and female (Gen 1:26-28).

This 'relationship' theme is developed in Genesis 2, where the creation of woman is described in detail. As in 1:26-28, the woman is similar to the man and yet different, and the two live in a unified relationship. It is also worth noting that this pattern is established *before the Fall*. Marriage and sex are part of God's good creation, not a consequence of the curse.

God sees that mankind needs relationship, and this is true in our experience as well. We humans are built for relationship, for interacting with each other. There are few human experiences more devastating than true loneliness.

As God creates a 'helper' for Adam in Genesis 2, we should note three things:

1. *Similarity*
The man needs a companion whose very essence is like his own. He needs a helper that is 'suitable' for him. And God meets this need by forming a helper out of the man's own body. In other words, for the relationship to be satisfactory, there must be similarity between the man and the woman.

2. *Diversity*
All the same, God does not create a second man. He creates a different, complementary being. There is similarity but there is also diversity—Adam and Eve, not Adam and Steve.

It is important to affirm this in light of some of the prevailing attitudes of our society. Many today want to eradicate any diversity between man and woman. It is argued that, apart from a few minor biological differences, there is no inherent difference between the sexes at all. They are not two different, complementary beings, but two identical beings. This does not accord with Genesis 2.

3 *Unity*

God intends that these two similar and yet diverse beings should become a unified whole. 'For this reason a man will leave his father and mother and be *united* to his wife and they will become *one flesh*' (Gen 2:24). This means not only setting up house together, but sexual unity. Just as they came from one flesh, so they again become one flesh in sex.

This tells us something of God's purpose for sex. Apart from the obvious reproductive function, sex is part of the bond between husband and wife; it unites them physically, but also at a more profound level. Sex is part of the glue that holds man and woman together in a unified relationship—the two of them ruling the world together as one mankind (cf. 1:26-28).

Of course, this unity is not very evident in our society. With something like forty per cent of marriages ending in divorce, and many of the rest battling on in discord and anguish, the Genesis ideal of a unified mankind seems distant. This is because we live *this* side of Genesis 3, where God pronounces a curse on mankind for their rebellion against him. The curse, as it affects marriage, is found in Genesis 3:16—'Your desire will be for your husband; and he will rule over you.'

The meaning of these enigmatic words becomes clear when we compare them with Genesis 4:7. God addresses Cain, saying, 'But if you do not do what is right, sin is crouching at your door; it *desires* to have you, but you must *master* it.'

In the Hebrew, these are the same words as in Genesis 3:16. That is, God's judgment is that the woman will desire to overthrow her husband, but he will rule over her. This is a powerful description of fallen human marriage. There is no longer unity and openness, but conflict. Each partner attempts to gain the ascendancy and get their own way—the wife by the sharpness of her tongue, the husband by the strength of his biceps.

Down through history, this has been the tragic reality of human relationships. Women have attacked men with their considerable emotional and verbal arsenal. Men have quashed the rebellion with brute force. Today, we recognise this and keep changing partners in a futile attempt to avoid the conflict.

Israel, God's Bride

As the Old Testament unfolds, the teaching on marriage goes in two distinct, though related, directions.

On the one hand, there is ethical instruction about the conduct of marriages. In a verse well-known to newly-weds, the Law makes provision for couples to enjoy themselves in their first year:

> If a man has recently married, he must not be sent to war or have any other duty laid on him. For one year he is to be free to stay at home and

bring happiness to the wife he has married.

Deuteronomy 24:5

Along the same lines, there are numerous injunctions to marital faithfulness and love, and warnings about the dangers of adultery. This passage from Proverbs is typical:

> The lips of an adulteress drip honey,
> and her speech is smoother than oil;
> but in the end she is bitter as gall,
> sharp as a double-edged sword...
> Drink water from your own cistern,
> running water from your own well...
> Let them be yours alone,
> never to be shared with strangers.
> May your fountain be blessed,
> and may you rejoice in the wife of your youth.
> A loving doe, a graceful deer—
> may her breasts satisfy you always,
> may you be ever captivated by her love.
>
> Proverbs 5:3-4, 15, 17-19

However, there is a second strand of thought in the Old Testament regarding marriage. Israel is described as being married to Yahweh, her God. The covenant relationship is often likened to a marriage, with God as the faithful, loving, long-suffering husband and Israel as the faithless, adulterous wife. The Book of Hosea is developed around this theme, but it also occurs in other places (e.g., Isa 54:5-6; 62:4-5; Jer 2:2; 3:14). As the nation of Israel declines, the prophets look forward to a time when God will make a new marriage contract with his wayward wife, Israel:

'It will not be like the covenant I made with their forefathers
when I took them by the hand to lead them out of Egypt,
because they broke my covenant,
though I was a husband to them,' declares the LORD.

Jerermiah 31:32

The Church, Christ's Bride

In the New Testament, these two strands of thought continue to run side by side, but with an important difference. Instead of the nation Israel being married to Yahweh, Christians are *betrothed to Christ*.

The process of becoming a Christian is described in terms of a courtship and marriage. Through hearing the one true gospel and placing our trust in it, we are betrothed (or engaged) to Christ (see 2 Cor 11:1-2). Paul is anxious that the Corinthians don't betray their husband-to-be by accepting some 'other Jesus' that is being preached to them. Paul wants to present the bride to her husband on the wedding day as a pure and spotless virgin. Much the same imagery is used in Revelation 19:6-9 as the multitudes sing:

'Hallelujah!
For our Lord God Almighty reigns.
Let us rejoice and be glad and give him glory!
For the wedding of the Lamb has come,

and his bride has made herself ready.
Fine linen, bright and clean, was given her to
wear.'
(Fine linen stands for the righteous acts of the
saints.)

Revelation 19:6-9

In Ephesians 5:22-33, the point is made even more
forcefully. Paul goes so far as to say that the
marriage between Christ and the church is the *real*
marriage, and that human marriages are models
of it:

> In this same way, husbands ought to love their
> wives as their own bodies. He who loves his wife
> loves himself. After all, no-one ever hated his
> own body, but he feeds and cares for it, just as
> Christ does the church—for we are members of
> his body. 'For this reason a man will leave his
> father and mother and be united to his wife, and
> the two will become one flesh.' *This is a profound
> mystery—but I am talking about Christ and the church.*
> However, each one of you also must love his wife
> as he loves himself, and the wife must respect her
> husband.
>
> Ephesians 5:28-33; emphasis mine

This is rather hard to grasp—indeed, Paul calls it a
'profound mystery'—but the point seems to be
this: that the one-flesh relationship established in
the Garden in Genesis 2 foreshadowed the coming
of Christ and his marriage to the church.

This means that every Christian is already engaged to be married—to Christ. This is the really

important marriage, and our preparation for it is holiness. Christ has paid the bride price to win us for himself, and we might even regard the gift of the Holy Spirit as an engagement ring, guaranteeing our participation in the wedding day at the end of time.

In the mean time, we are to prepare ourselves for the wedding by putting on 'holiness' and 'righteous acts' as our bridal clothes. Christ wants a spotless bride, without blemish, and for this reason he died for his bride to wash her clean of sin.

Holy Matrimony

What does all this mean for our earthly marriages? Are they obsolete, or even sinful, now that we are 'engaged' to Christ? In the past, some Christians have concluded this and have abstained from marriage altogether. (They should have read 1 Timothy 4:1-4 where Paul blasts the false teaching of those who 'forbid people to marry'.)

Perhaps the Christians in first century Corinth thought something like this, for in his first letter to them, Paul addresses the issue of marriage and celibacy.

> Now for the matters you wrote about: It is good for a man not to marry. But since there is so much immorality, each man should have his own wife, and each woman her own husband. The husband should fulfil his marital duty to his wife, and

likewise the wife to her husband. The wife's body does not belong to her alone but also to her husband. In the same way, the husband's body does not belong to him alone but also to his wife. Do not deprive each other except by mutual consent and for a time, so that you may devote yourselves to prayer. Then come together again so that Satan will not tempt you because of your lack of self-control. I say this as a concession, not as a command. I wish that all men were as I am. But each man has his own gift from God; one has this gift, another has that.

Now to the unmarried and the widows I say: It is good for them to stay unmarried, as I am. But if they cannot control themselves, they should marry, for it is better to marry than to burn with passion.

1 Corinthians 7:1-9

We should note the following:

- Christians are quite free to marry or remain single—there is no sin involved in either course.
- One of the primary motivations for marriage (in fact, the only one given in this passage) is sex. If we find we cannot control our sexual desires, we should marry for 'it is better to marry than to burn with passion' (7:9). This advice goes against our grain, but perhaps this is because we have a romantic view of marriage and an unromantic view of sex.
- We are free to marry or not, but we are *not* free about holiness. We are to flee immoral-

ity (6:18), for our bodies are home to God's own Spirit. Whether married or single, holiness is the crucial issue. It is far more important than marriage. In fact, the pursuit of holiness lies behind the advice about 'burning with passion'. If our holiness is under threat from sexual temptation, then we should marry lest our holiness be compromised.

- This all fits with what Paul says in the passages we looked at earlier. The ultimate marriage, the marriage that really counts, is our marriage to Christ, and our preparation for that marriage is holiness. Therefore, the guiding principle for all our behaviour in this life, including marriage, is holiness. If we do marry, then once again the important factor is not so much *whom* we marry, but the quality or holiness of the marriage. We see this in Ephesians 5:22-33, where Christ and his holy church serve as a model for the sacrificial love and submission of human marriage.

Decisions We Make

All this is quite radical. It cuts across the prevailing tone of our culture so completely that it challenges our willingness to believe. Can we bring ourselves to believe and act on the idea that holiness is a higher priority than marriage? Are we prepared to heed God's guidance and follow?

Let's look at some of the practical decisions we are faced with and at how God's radical guidance affects them.

1. Whether to marry

The first and most basic decision is whether to marry at all. This is a genuine choice, and one which too few Christians consider. 1 Corinthians 7 makes it clear that marriage is a matter of indifference for us, and that there are distinct advantages in being single, especially in doing the Lord's work. Yet those who do not have the gift of being able to control their sexual appetites should marry with a clear conscience.

Many modern Christians are so committed to the idea of marriage that they will marry an unbeliever rather than remain single. People in Bible times rarely had much choice of marriage partner, but where there was a choice, they were to marry a believer (see 1 Cor 7:39). If we marry an unbeliever in our desperation to marry, we have compromised the holiness of our true marriage to Christ.

Holiness is the key, and that is what Paul is concerned about in 1 Corinthians 7. If we are aflame with passion and our holiness is under threat, then we should marry. If God has gifted us to cope with the strains of the single life, then that is better by far.

This is a simple, straightforward choice in theory. In practice, it can be a little more complicated, especially for women. It is comparatively easy to decide, 'Yes, I want to get married.' Finding an eligible Christian partner can sometimes be more difficult.

We should bear in mind that Paul's instructions in 1 Corinthians 7 were delivered to people for whom 'choice of partner' was quite limited. Most marriages in the ancient world were arranged. There was none of the complex system of romantic manoeuvring and courting that we are 'blessed' with. In light of this, perhaps we need to do three things:

- Recognise that finding a partner in our society is not always easy, and pray for God to provide us with someone.
- Wait patiently and trust that God has our best interests at heart.
- Be less fussy. We are greatly influenced by the Hollywood myth-making machine. Most of us have some vision of the perfect wife/husband, and we hold out waiting for her/him to come along. We need to be honest with ourselves. Is it that there are no godly women/men to marry, or is it that there are none who have the particular looks and personal charm that we are after?

2. *The Limits*
If we decide to marry, then the Bible gives us

some clear guidelines. Some aspects of our choice
of partner are simple questions of right and
wrong—in other words, they are questions of holiness. The person we choose must be:

- not a blood relative;
- free to marry (that is, not already married);
- a Christian;
- of the opposite sex.

These are the limits of a godly choice. Anyone
who satisfies these criteria is a right choice of
marriage partner. We can marry someone who
fits this checklist confident that we are acting in
line with God's revealed will.

The opposite is also true. If a prospective partner fails one of these tests, then there is no further
guidance needed. They are a *wrong* choice. There
is no sense praying or seeking God's will further—
God has already given the answer in unambiguous
terms: it is wrong.

Obviously, this opens up a large pool of potential marriage partners, and it would be *right* to
marry any of them. Is it as simple as that? Almost,
but not quite.

3. Godly Wisdom

In Chapter 8, we drew a distinction between right/
wrong decisions and wise/unwise decisions.
Whether a Christian should marry a non-Christian
is a simple case of right and wrong. However,

given that there are a number of people who fall into the *right* category, we should exercise godly *wisdom* in making our choice.

What wisdom does the Bible give for choosing a marriage partner?

From passages like Ephesians 5 and 1 Peter 3, we learn that the ideal husband is tall, handsome, athletic, charming, intelligent, masterful, and one or two levels higher in the socio-economic strata. At least, that's what people seem to learn, since that's the kind of husband most Christian women seem to be looking for. The ideal husband of the Bible is quite different: he is gentle, loving and sacrificial. He's the sort of person who looks out for other peoples' interests, who is keen to submit to Christ and has a living, growing relationship with him.

Likewise, the godly wife is gentle and quiet in spirit. She has the inner beauty and responsiveness that flow from her relationship with God.

These are the characteristics of the godly husband/wife. This is the sort of partner that makes for a wise choice.

4. *The World's Wisdom*

The non-Christian world has a lot to say about love and marriage. And some of it is quite helpful. Marriage and sex counsellors can provide real help for struggling couples in numerous ways.

However, much of what the world says about marriage—and especially its guidelines for choice

of partner—is disastrous.   We are taught from
childhood that when we grow up we will meet that
special 'someone', fall in love and get married.
'And live happily ever after' used to be tacked onto
the end of that sequence, but not any longer. These
days it's more like: 'And live happily for a couple
of years at least until we tire of each other and
get a divorce.'

Physical appearance and attractiveness play a
large part in worldly partner choice, as does an
elusive characteristic called 'compatibility'. What
'compatibility' is exactly, no-one seems to know.
One thing is certain: we have no way of knowing
whether we will still be 'compatible' with our partner in ten, twenty or fifty years time.   People
change a lot in twenty years.

The Bible's emphasis on godliness, humility
and love, cuts right across the world's wisdom.
This makes wise decision-making in this area difficult, because we are often going against the attitudes and ideas that we have been raised on.

5. *Deciding to be Godly Before the Event*
There is danger inherent in trying to make a wise
choice of partner—the focus is always on the godliness of the *other* person. We scan the available
pool of candidates, looking for that special someone. With the Bible's wisdom now on board, at
least we are looking for a godly someone. But we
are so busy looking at everyone else that we forget
to look at ourselves.

One of the most important decisions we can make in preparation for marriage is to be godly *ourselves*. We need to ask: what sort of husband/ wife would I make? We need to make a realistic comparison between ourselves and the model held up in Ephesians 5 and 1 Peter 3. How do we stack up? Rather than concentrating solely on our search for the perfect partner, we would do well to work on our lives, our own character and godliness. This will have a far greater impact on our future marriages than the discovery of Miss/ Mr Right. If you want a long and successful marriage, start working on it now by becoming like Christ.

6. Deciding to be Godly After the Event

The ironic thing about marriage is that most people think that the really big decision is the choice of partner. Get that right, and the marriage will be blessed. Get that wrong, and you live with your mistake for the rest of your life. This is not only quite contrary to what God thinks, it is also incredibly naive.

Marriages survive or fail on the daily growth and godliness of the partners. Marriage is hard work. It takes commitment, persistence and an ongoing desire to love the other person unconditionally. Choosing the 'perfect' partner doesn't ensure a good marriage. Wisely choosing a godly partner helps. The daily decision to keep loving your partner, even when it hurts, is what makes a marriage last and grow.

This, then, is the crucial decision affecting marriage—the decision to keep your marriage promises each day, to love your partner regardless of the circumstances, to honour and cherish each other, to grow like Christ together over ten, twenty, fifty years. This deliberate, intentional choice—to keep loving even when you don't feel like it—is the most difficult choice of all, and by far the most important.

If all these decisions about marriage seem like a lot to cope with, perhaps we should offer a word of encouragement. You might remember the first of our propositions about how God guides, back in Chapter 7: *God, in his sovereignty, uses everything to guide us 'behind the scenes'.*

We need to remind ourselves that God is our great Father and Shepherd. He looks after us, and guides us according to his purposes in ways that we can sometimes only guess at. We can be assured that he is working 'behind the scenes' for our good in our choice of marriage partner.

Indeed, there will come a time when we will know, for a certainty, that we have found the marriage partner that God has chosen for us. What is that time? The first morning of our honeymoon.

12

The Last Word

Eleven chapters ago, we started with an arrogant title and a promise of discovering the secrets of God's guidance. We hope that by now you've realised that God's guidance is no secret. It is open and clear and available for anyone who cares to listen.

But what about our arrogant title? We chose this title for two reasons, and outlining those reasons is perhaps a good way to conclude.

The first reason is negative. One of our main points has been that the popular approach to 'guidance' is seriously flawed. The modern teaching about 'the peace' and 'fleeces' and 'confirmatory signs' turns guidance into a complex process of trying to discover God's special plan for your life. We have attempted to show that this search for special guidance is both unbiblical and unnecessary.

We hope that Christians will give up discussing guidance (as the word is usually used) and spend more time discussing godliness and obedience to God's revealed will. It is perhaps too much to hope for, but we pray that this book will indeed be the last word on 'guidance'.

The second reason for our title is more positive. It is summarised in the opening sentence of the Book of Hebrews:

> In the past God spoke to our forefathers through the prophets at many times and in various ways, but in these last days he has spoken to us by his Son...

This is the positive argument of our book in a nutshell. God has chosen to speak in many and varied ways in the past, but in Christ he has uttered a comprehensive and final word for the last days in which we live. In Christ, God has brought all his plans to fulfilment (see Matt 5:17; 2 Cor 1:20). In him, the very fulness of God dwells (Col 2:9). He is the exact representation of God's being (Heb 1:3). The New Testament reveals this Christ to us, and calls on us to repent and put our trust in him.

The New Testament also urges us not to go elsewhere for revelation or to 'move on' from Christ. He is all we know, and all we need to know. Paul's exhortation to the Colossians is typical:

> Just as you received Christ Jesus as Lord, continue
> to live in him, rooted and built up in him, strength-
> ened in the faith as you were taught, and over-
> flowing with thankfulness.
>
> Colossians 2:6-7

Those who advocate a specially revealed 'will of
God' for each Christian inadvertently undercut the
majesty and finality of God's revelation in Christ.
God has given us 'everything we need for life
and godliness through our knowledge of him
who called us by his own glory and goodness' (2
Pet 1:3). God has not left us in the dark, nor has he
kept back part of his revelation for us to discover
through various quasi-mystical techniques.

Jesus Christ is God's *Last Word on Guidance*.
Christ fulfils the eternal plan of God to redeem his
people and lead them home.   He is the Good
Shepherd, whose words are life. In listening to his
voice, and following it, we receive sure and marvellous guidance. What more do we need?